AF490642

The Roadmap to Fire Behavior

Eric J. Neal

Published by Eric J. Neal, 2024.

While every precaution has been taken in the preparation of this book, the publisher assumes no responsibility for errors or omissions, or for damages resulting from the use of the information contained herein.

THE ROADMAP TO FIRE BEHAVIOR

First edition. December 12, 2024.

Copyright © 2024 Eric J. Neal.

ISBN: 979-8230851264

Written by Eric J. Neal.

Table of Contents

This Book is dedicated to the brave men and women who answer the call, day and night, to protect our communities. To the fire personnel and responders who run toward danger when others flee, your courage, commitment, and unwavering dedication are the backbone of fire safety and emergency response. Your constant pursuit of knowledge, skill, and excellence ensures that when lives are at stake, you are prepared to face the challenges ahead.

May this guide serve as a small contribution to your continued growth, a reminder that the journey of learning never ends. As you learn, adapt, and innovate, know that your efforts are deeply appreciated by all who rely on your expertise and bravery. Your tireless work saves lives, protects property, and keeps communities safe. Thank you for your service, your resilience, and for always striving to be the best in your field.

This is for you, the dedicated heroes who make a difference every day.

Introduction

Imagine you're standing at the edge of a vast, roaring river. The water's movement is unpredictable—sometimes calm and serene, sometimes wild and tumultuous. You can't control this river, but you can learn to navigate it with skill and precision. Welcome to the world of firefighting, where understanding the ever-changing nature of fire is akin to mastering the flow of a mighty river.

Firefighting is more than just a job; it's a calling, a commitment to protect lives and property from one of the most formidable forces of nature: fire. As a firefighter, you are the frontline defense against this relentless adversary, and every day presents a new challenge that tests not only your physical prowess but also your mental acuity. This book is designed for those who have taken that oath to serve and wish to deepen their understanding of fire dynamics—a crucial component in the art of firefighting.

The heart of firefighting lies in one's ability to interpret and react to the behavior of fire. Fire is not merely an element to be extinguished; it is a living, breathing entity influenced by a myriad of factors. These factors include the type of materials involved (the fuel), the heat present, the availability of oxygen, and the surrounding environment. Each ignites, fuels, and shapes the fire in ways that can alter its path and intensity. Understanding these interactions is essential for effectively combating flames and safeguarding yourself and others from harm.

Envision yourself at the scene of a fire, the smoke thick in the air, the heat palpable through your protective gear. It's here that the concepts we're about to explore become your greatest allies. Grasping the principles of fire behavior allows you to read the environment as if it were a book, predicting how the fire will behave next and devising a strategy tailored to that particular scenario. Whether faced with a towering inferno in a high-rise building, a blaze consuming a rural home, or a wildfire encroaching upon civilization, adapting your tactics is key.

The variability of fire means that no two fires are alike, each harboring its own set of challenges. Your approach must be dynamic, drawing upon a reservoir of knowledge that underpins every decision you make in the heat of the moment. Detailed within these pages are the core concepts of fire behavior—how it grows, spreads, and eventually decays.

Fire growth begins with ignition, this initial stage where sparks catch, and flames take hold. Here, our focus will be materials and the conditions that facilitate ignition. Following ignition, we enter the realm of fire spread—how flames leap from object to object, room to room. This is dictated by the combination of fuel types and configurations, the architecture of the environment, and the presence of drafts or ventilation, enabling flames to thrive or falter.

Grasping these processes helps tailor responses to diverse environments. Tackling a blazing residential structure differs significantly from managing a fire within a commercial space laden with hazardous materials. Wildland-urban interfaces pose further complications, blending natural fuels with human-made structures, demanding careful consideration of ecological and safety factors.

As an integral part of fire dynamics, preparation equips us for the unique challenges each incident presents. Training sharpens skills, fostering reflexive actions when seconds matter. Situational awareness becomes second nature, guiding decisions amid chaos. Safety protocols form the bedrock of every operation, ensuring team unity and coherent execution.

Throughout this guide, you'll find insights into the multifaceted challenges of firefighting and practical techniques to enhance your readiness. As complex as the science of fire may seem, it boils down to simple truths: knowledge empowers, and preparation prevails. Mastering fire behavior provides the tactical advantage necessary not only for survival but for triumph over the ever-evolving dance of flame and shadow.

This introduction serves as a gateway to a deeper understanding of the world of fire dynamics. By undertaking this journey, you equip yourself with the tools needed to face the mercurial nature of fire with confidence and precision. Armed with these insights, you can navigate the river of fire, steering toward safety and success while protecting others.

As you embark on this exploration of fire behavior and firefighter preparation, remember that you do so not only for the fulfillment of personal curiosity but for the safety and security of those depending on your expertise. Your community looks to you as a guardian—resilient, knowledgeable, and prepared for whatever challenges arise. Embrace this opportunity to enrich your understanding and hone your skills.

Together, let us delve into the depths of fire dynamics, uncovering the secrets that lie within the flames. Let us prepare ourselves to meet the demands of one of the most perilous and rewarding professions. In understanding fire, in learning to anticipate and control this powerful force, you fortify your ability to stand between destruction and refuge. Ready yourself for the journey ahead, as this river of fire awaits your mastery.

Chapter 1: Introduction to Fire Dynamics

Understanding fire dynamics is essential for those on the front lines battling blazes. It involves a deep dive into the lifecycle of fires, starting with ignition and ending with effective extinguishment. The intricacies of how fires start, spread, and can be controlled form the backbone of safety strategies and tactical firefighting. This discipline isn't just about academic knowledge; it's about enhancing the practical capabilities of firefighters to tackle life-threatening situations effectively. With each phase of a fire presenting unique challenges, comprehending these core principles directly impacts the effectiveness and safety of firefighting operations.

In this chapter, we delve into the scientific fundamentals that influence every aspect of fire behavior. Readers will explore the chemistry behind combustion—how different materials react and contribute to fire spread—and the role of the Fire Triangle and Tetrahedron in sustaining flames. The mechanisms of heat transfer—through conduction, convection, and radiation—will be examined to understand their effects during a fire event. Furthermore, environmental conditions such as weather and building designs will be highlighted for their significant impact on fire dynamics. By integrating insights from various interdisciplinary fields like chemistry and fluid mechanics, this chapter aims to equip firefighters with the knowledge necessary to predict fire behaviors accurately. Additionally, readers will uncover how these principles inform risk assessment, resource allocation, and the development of strategic interventions, ensuring both firefighter and civilian safety. Through this comprehensive overview, the chapter seeks to bridge theoretical understanding with practical application, preparing firefighters for the dynamic challenges they encounter.

Overview of Fire Dynamics

Fire dynamics is a critical discipline focused on understanding the lifecycle of fires, from ignition to extinguishment. It encompasses the study of how fires start, spread, and are controlled — each phase presenting unique challenges and requiring specific knowledge to manage effectively. For firefighters, mastering these elements is not merely academic; it is a matter of life and death. Properly understanding fire dynamics can lead to more effective firefighting strategies, enhancing safety outcomes substantially.

When we talk about fire dynamics, we refer to the scientific principles that dictate how fires develop. This includes an examination of the chemical reactions involved in combustion and how those reactions influence fire behavior. At its core, fire dynamics integrates several key fields such as chemistry, fluid mechanics, heat transfer, and material science to provide a comprehensive overview of fire phenomena (Thompson, 2010).

One crucial aspect is examining how fires ignite and spread in various environments. Knowing these processes can help firefighters predict potential hazards and prepare for them effectively. Notably, fires require three primary components to sustain: fuel, oxygen, and heat. This basic requirement is often represented by the Fire Triangle. However, in modern firefighting, understanding has evolved to include the Fire Tetrahedron, which adds the element of an uninhibited chemical reaction necessary for maintaining a fire.

Fuel properties play a significant role in determining fire behavior. Different fuels have varied combustion rates and energy outputs, influencing how quickly a fire can spread. Certain materials may burn at higher temperatures or release more energy, necessitating a tactical adjustment in firefighting approaches. By studying these properties through the lens of fire dynamics, firefighters can anticipate fire spread and adopt strategies to control it efficiently.

Heat transfer is another vital concept within fire dynamics. Heat moves through conduction, convection, and radiation, affecting everything from the surrounding atmosphere to structural stability during a fire event. Understanding these mechanisms allows firefighters to predict how heat will move and where it might pose the greatest threat. For example, radiant heat from a fire can preheat nearby fuel sources, accelerating fire spread if not adequately managed.

Environmental factors, including weather conditions, building design, and ventilation, also greatly influence fire dynamics. Wind can drive fire growth unpredictably, while structures with limited ventilation may experience a buildup of heat and smoke, leading to potential backdrafts or flashovers. Knowledge of these variables enables firefighters to modify their tactics dynamically, ensuring they adapt to changing fire conditions swiftly and safely.

The significance of fire dynamics in firefighting extends beyond immediate tactical advantages. By integrating these principles into training programs, firefighters enhance their situational awareness and decision-making capabilities under pressure. Educational initiatives that focus on the complex interplay of factors driving fire behavior foster a culture of safety and preparedness, equipping firefighters with the tools needed to minimize risks.

Effective interventions rely heavily on predicting fire behavior accurately. Techniques derived from fire dynamics can help identify potential collapse zones, identify optimal points for venting smoke, and assist in devising evacuation routes. These predictions are made using models that simulate real-world scenarios, offering valuable insights into the consequences of different actions in fire situations (*Unlocking the Secrets of Fire Behavior: A Vital Evolution in Firefighting Tactics*, 2024).

Furthermore, fire dynamics provides firefighters with the knowledge required for risk assessment. Evaluating a scene through this lens ensures that resources are allocated wisely, and firefighting efforts are focused where they are most needed. This proactive approach reduces the likelihood of injuries and fatalities among both firefighters and civilians.

Incorporating fire dynamics into everyday firefighting practice represents a commitment to continuous improvement. As the field evolves, new research findings should be consistently integrated into strategies, ensuring that firefighters remain at the forefront of safety and efficiency. Bridging the gap between academic research and practical application empowers firefighters to respond more adeptly to the diverse challenges they face in their line of duty.

Basic Principles of Combustion

In the realm of fire dynamics, understanding the fundamentals of combustion is crucial for both preventative measures and effective responses. Combustion, at its core, is a chemical reaction that involves oxygen and a fuel source combining to produce heat and light. This process is fundamental to understanding how fires ignite and sustain themselves. By delving into this reaction, firefighters can grasp how different elements interact to create the flames they face.

At the heart of combustion lies the Fire Triangle, a concept used to illustrate the three essential components needed for a fire to exist: fuel, heat, and oxygen. Each element of the triangle plays a vital role in sustaining a fire. Fuel serves as the substance that burns, heat is necessary to raise the fuel to its ignition temperature, and oxygen supports the chemical reactions that keep the fire burning. It's important to understand that removing any one of these elements will extinguish the fire, making the Fire Triangle a foundational tool in both preventing and fighting fires.

However, the simplicity of the Fire Triangle doesn't encompass all aspects of what makes combustion possible. This is where the concept expands into the Fire Tetrahedron. The Fire Tetrahedron introduces a fourth element: the chemical chain reaction. This addition explains how once a fire is ignited; it can sustain itself without any additional external heat. The chemical chain reaction represents the series of exothermic reactions that continue to produce heat, thus maintaining the combustion process. This aspect of the tetrahedron underlines the complexity of fires and challenges firefighters to consider not just the superficial elements but the underlying chemical processes when tackling a blaze.

Recognizing the interplay of these components is not merely an academic exercise; it has practical implications on the front lines of firefighting. For instance, understanding how the absence of any element from the Fire Triangle or Fire Tetrahedron results in fire extinction can guide strategies for fire suppression. In practice, firefighters implement this knowledge by using water to cool the fire (removing heat), cutting off the oxygen supply with foams or blankets, or starving the fire of fuel through controlled methods like firebreaks.

A comprehensive understanding of combustion also aids in anticipating how fires might behave under varying conditions. Different fuels have distinct combustion properties, influencing how quickly they ignite, how intensely they burn, and how challenging they are to extinguish. Firefighters equipped with this knowledge can make informed decisions about which tactics to use in containing a fire and preventing its spread.

Environmental factors further complicate combustion and fire behavior. Variables such as humidity, wind speed, and terrain can alter how fuel, heat, and oxygen come together. For instance, winds can provide additional oxygen while dispersing embers, facilitating rapid fire spread. Similarly, dry conditions increase the likelihood of ignition. Here, an understanding of combustion principles enables predicting fire behavior more accurately and tailoring firefighting approaches accordingly.

As firefighters advance in their careers, this foundational understanding of combustion becomes integral to their training and operations. Training programs emphasize these concepts, ensuring that every member of a firefighting team comprehends how to apply the theories of the Fire Triangle and Tetrahedron practically. Knowledge of combustion is not just theoretical but forms the backbone of tactical decision-making during high-pressure situations.

Furthermore, new technology continues to emerge, offering sophisticated tools for monitoring and controlling combustion during firefighting efforts. Advanced sensors detect variations in heat and smoke, allowing firefighters to assess the situation more accurately and swiftly. This technological edge complements traditional knowledge, enabling better prediction, control, and extinguishment of fires.

The Role of Fire Dynamics in Firefighting

The understanding of fire dynamics is fundamental to enhancing firefighting practices. By comprehending how fires behave, firefighters can make informed decisions that improve both their safety and the effectiveness of their response efforts. One of the primary benefits of this knowledge is its use in conducting accurate risk assessments and maintaining situational awareness. Risk assessment is an essential process in managing fire-related emergencies, as it evaluates potential threats and guides the preparation for unforeseen outcomes. Traditional methods like quantitative risk analysis (QRA) employ tools such as fault tree analysis (FTA) and event tree analysis (ETA) to systematically assess these risks (Liu et al., 2024). Incorporating fire dynamics into these analyses allows responders to anticipate how a fire might evolve, thus refining emergency readiness.

Understanding fire dynamics also significantly influences strategic decision-making in firefighting operations. Knowing how different factors affect fire behavior enables commanders to allocate resources judiciously and choose appropriate tactical approaches. For instance, recognizing the potential spread rate of a fire helps in deciding where to deploy water hoses and additional manpower to prevent expansion to sensitive areas. Such strategic planning is crucial for ensuring that resources are used efficiently without compromising the safety of the crew or the affected individuals. Fire dynamics knowledge can inform decisions about when to retreat and reassess strategies and when to aggressively tackle the fire head-on, ultimately shaping the outcome of the firefighting effort.

Moreover, insight into fire spread rates and patterns plays a vital role in planning safe evacuation routes and containment measures. A thorough understanding of fire dynamics allows firefighters to predict the direction and speed of a fire's spread, which is critical for determining the safest escape paths for both occupants and rescue personnel. The layout of a building or outdoor environment, combined with environmental conditions such as wind speed and fuel availability, affects this spread. This dynamic nature means that evacuation plans must be adaptable, reflecting real-time changes in fire behavior to ensure all individuals can evacuate safely. Dynamic methodologies, such as those developed by Liu et al. (2024), account for evolving fire scenarios by simulating various outcomes, thereby providing a comprehensive view of the possible challenges during evacuations.

Fire dynamics also enhance firefighter preparedness through targeted training programs. By incorporating detailed simulations and real-life scenarios based on fire dynamics research, training can become more effective at preparing firefighters for actual incidents. Simulations using tools like Fire Dynamics Simulator (FDS) and evacuation modeling software provide valuable insights into the interaction between fire products and human behavior (Liu et al., 2024). These insights enable training regimens to go beyond traditional techniques, emphasizing the importance of understanding fire growth patterns, toxic smoke hazards, and heat impacts. Such programs educate firefighters not only on how to extinguish fires but also on protecting themselves and others from the dangers posed by high temperatures and hazardous materials encountered during fires (*Fire Safety in High-Risk Settings | American Trade Mark Co.*, 2024).

Guidelines within these training programs are crucial for ensuring that all firefighters receive consistent and reliable instruction on handling high-risk situations. Emphasizing protocols such as regular risk assessments and safety drills helps reinforce the necessary precautions firefighters must take in dynamic environments. Additionally, utilizing incident command boards and emergency management principles bolsters the ability to track personnel and manage special hazards effectively (*Fire Safety in High-Risk Settings | American Trade Mark Co.*, 2024). By standardizing these guidelines across departments, the level of preparedness among firefighters nationwide can be elevated, reducing the likelihood of injury or fatalities while improving response outcomes.

Summary and Reflections

Understanding the fundamental principles of fire dynamics is essential for effective firefighting and improving safety. Throughout this chapter, we have explored how fires begin, spread, and are controlled, emphasizing the necessity of mastering these elements. We discussed the critical role of the Fire Triangle and Fire Tetrahedron in understanding combustion, highlighting the three primary components needed for a fire to sustain itself: fuel, oxygen, and heat. By integrating knowledge from fields such as chemistry, fluid mechanics, and material science, firefighters can predict fire behavior and adapt their strategies accordingly. This comprehension not only aids in extinguishing fires but also enhances situational awareness and decision-making during emergencies.

Incorporating these lessons into everyday firefighting practices leads to more informed risk assessments and strategic decisions. Understanding how various factors influence fire spread allows for better planning of resource allocation, evacuation routes, and containment measures. Training programs that incorporate fire dynamics provide firefighters with a detailed understanding of fire growth patterns and toxic smoke hazards, preparing them to face real-life incidents effectively. By continuing to integrate the latest research findings into training and operational strategies, firefighters can ensure they remain at the forefront of safety and efficiency, ultimately minimizing risks to themselves and civilians alike.

Chapter 1 Test Questions and Answers
What is fire dynamics?
Fire dynamics is the study of how fires start, spread, and are controlled, integrating principles from chemistry, fluid mechanics, heat transfer, and material science.

Why is understanding fire dynamics critical for firefighters?
It enhances situational awareness, informs decision-making, and improves tactical strategies, ultimately increasing firefighter safety and operational success.

What are the three essential components of the Fire Triangle?
Fuel, heat, and oxygen.

What is the key addition in the Fire Tetrahedron compared to the Fire Triangle?
The Fire Tetrahedron adds the element of an uninhibited chemical chain reaction, which sustains combustion.

How does removing one element of the Fire Triangle extinguish a fire?
Removing heat (cooling with water), oxygen (suffocating with foam or blankets), or fuel (isolating flammable materials) will stop the combustion process.

What is combustion?
Combustion is a chemical reaction that produces heat and light by combining oxygen with a fuel source.

How can environmental conditions influence combustion?
Factors such as humidity, wind speed, and terrain can alter how fuel, heat, and oxygen interact, impacting fire spread.

Why is the chemical chain reaction in the Fire Tetrahedron significant?
It explains how fires can sustain themselves without continuous external heat input.

How do different fuels impact fire behavior?

Fuels vary in combustion rates and energy output, which affects fire intensity and spread speed.

What are three common methods of heat transfer in a fire?

Conduction, convection, and radiation.

How does radiant heat contribute to fire spread?

Radiant heat can preheat nearby fuels, making them more likely to ignite and accelerate fire spread.

What role does ventilation play in fire behavior?

Limited ventilation can cause heat and smoke buildup, increasing the risk of backdrafts or flashovers.

Why is wind a significant environmental factor in fire spread?

Wind can rapidly supply additional oxygen and spread embers, accelerating fire growth.

What are the primary benefits of fire dynamics knowledge in risk assessment?

It helps predict fire behavior, identify collapse zones, and determine effective evacuation routes.

How can fire dynamics improve firefighter tactics?

By understanding heat movement, material combustion rates, and fire spread patterns, firefighters can better allocate resources and adjust strategies.

How do training simulations help firefighters apply fire dynamics knowledge?

Simulations using tools like Fire Dynamics Simulator (FDS) allow firefighters to practice real-life scenarios, improving their decision-making skills.

What role do evacuation modeling systems play in fire preparedness?

They predict potential fire spread patterns and identify safe evacuation routes.

How can incident command boards improve firefighter safety?

They help track personnel locations, manage hazards, and ensure efficient communication during emergencies.

Why is continuous learning essential in fire dynamics?

Fire behavior research evolves, and integrating new findings helps firefighters stay updated on best practices for safety and efficiency.

How do firefighters use fire dynamics to predict potential collapse zones?

By analyzing heat movement, structural stability, and fire progression, firefighters can anticipate unsafe areas and adjust their positioning accordingly.

Chapter 2: Knowing the Fire Triangle and Tetrahedron

Understanding the dynamics of fire is a crucial component for effective firefighting. This chapter delves into two key frameworks that guide this understanding: the fire triangle and the fire tetrahedron. The fire triangle—comprising fuel, heat, and oxygen—presents a foundational model explaining how fires ignite and sustain themselves. Each element plays an essential role, and grasping their interplay provides valuable insights into fire behavior. With a clear understanding of these components, firefighters can strategize more effectively to extinguish flames, ensuring their safety and minimizing damage. However, the complexities of modern-day fires necessitate a deeper exploration beyond this basic framework.

The chapter further introduces the fire tetrahedron, which expands upon the fire triangle by integrating the critical fourth element of the chemical chain reaction. This addition offers a more comprehensive perspective on fire dynamics, reflecting the intricate processes involved in sustaining combustion. By examining the chemical reactions within a fire, the fire tetrahedron equips firefighters with the knowledge to combat fires more efficiently by targeting all elements at play. As such, this section underscores the importance of adopting advanced strategies tailored to contemporary challenges posed by complex fire scenarios, including those involving synthetic materials and new technologies. Through this nuanced approach, the chapter aims to empower firefighters with enhanced tools and techniques to manage diverse and dynamic fire situations effectively.

Understanding the Fire Triangle

In understanding fire dynamics, recognizing the fundamental components necessary for fire ignition and spread is crucial. These components—fuel, heat, and oxygen—form the basis of the fire triangle, and each plays a vital role in the process of combustion.

Fuel is one of the essential pillars of the fire triangle. It serves as a combustible material that acts as the primary source of energy for sustaining fire (Blazequel, 2024). Fuels can vary widely, ranging from natural substances such as wood, paper, and leaves to synthetic ones like gasoline and plastic. Each type of fuel has unique properties, burning at different rates and temperatures. For instance, wood burns slowly with a steady flame, while gasoline ignites rapidly with intense heat. Understanding the nature of the fuel involved is critical for firefighters when assessing a fire's potential behavior and planning an effective response. Moreover, the flashover phenomenon highlights the significance of fuel in fire dynamics. In a flashover, all combustible materials in a room reach their ignition temperature simultaneously, leading to a sudden and intense outbreak of flames (Blazequel, 2024).

Heat is another indispensable component needed for fire ignition and spread. Heat acts as the catalyst, elevating the fuel to its ignition temperature, allowing the combustion process to occur (University of South Carolina, 2019). Without sufficient heat, even the most combustible materials will not ignite. Sources of heat can be varied, including open flames, electrical sparks, or friction. Once a fire has started, it generates its own heat, creating a self-sustaining cycle that allows the fire to grow and spread. The ability of heat to propagate through conduction, convection, and radiation means that it can transfer its energy to nearby combustible materials, causing them to ignite and further feeding the fire. This aspect of heat underscores the importance of controlling its sources to prevent unintended fires and minimize damage during firefighting efforts.

Oxygen plays a pivotal role in maintaining combustion and supporting the chemical reactions within a fire. Oxygen is present in the air we breathe, making it readily available in most environments. When a fire begins, oxygen molecules diffuse into the fire zone, reacting with the fuel to release energy and generate more heat (University of South Carolina, 2019). This continuous supply of oxygen maintains the combustion process and supports the growth of the fire. The concentration of oxygen influences how fiercely a fire burns; the more oxygen available, the faster and hotter the fire will grow. Conversely, reducing the oxygen supply can effectively extinguish a fire, which is a common strategy employed in using fire extinguishers or smothering techniques. By depriving a fire of oxygen, its combustion process is disrupted, leading to its eventual extinction.

The interplay between these three elements—fuel, heat, and oxygen—ultimately determines the behavior and intensity of the fire. The relationship is dynamic and interdependent; changes in one component can significantly impact the others. For example, increasing the heat can cause more fuel to ignite, while additional oxygen can make the fire burn more intensely. Firefighters must assess this interplay to develop effective strategies for managing fires. Understanding how these elements interact allows for accurate predictions of fire behavior, essential for ensuring the safety of both firefighters and the public. In uncontrolled conditions, such as wildfires, this knowledge becomes even more critical as factors like wind and terrain can alter the availability and interaction of fuel, heat, and oxygen, making containment challenging.

By focusing on the fire triangle's components, firefighters gain valuable insights into how to approach and tackle different types of fires. Strategies can be tailored based on which element is most feasible to manage or mitigate in a given situation. For instance, removing accessible fuel sources or controlling heat generation can help limit a fire's spread. Additionally, understanding the oxygen concentration in structures or natural environments can assist in determining the best methods for oxygen reduction interventions. Ultimately, mastering the dynamics of the fire triangle equips firefighters with the tools to execute precise and effective responses to fires, minimizing risks and enhancing safety in high-stakes situations.

The Fire Tetrahedron

Fire dynamics are a crucial area of study for firefighters and safety professionals, as these principles form the foundation for effective fire management and control strategies. At the heart of this understanding lies the concept of the fire tetrahedron, which builds upon the traditional fire triangle by introducing a vital fourth element: the chemical chain reaction. This addition is not just an academic exercise but a critical lens through which we can more precisely predict and control fire behavior.

The chemical chain reaction is fundamental to sustaining combustion. In essence, it perpetuates the fire cycle by generating heat, which in turn promotes the further breakdown of fuel. This continuous loop ensures that once a fire begins, it maintains its momentum until one or more elements are removed. Recognizing how this reaction works is essential for firefighters aiming to disrupt these processes effectively. By breaking the chain reaction, either through chemical extinguishers or other suppression techniques, we can halt a fire's progress more efficiently.

Furthermore, understanding the tetrahedron has transformed our ability to predict fire behavior. While the traditional fire triangle—comprising heat, fuel, and oxygen—provides a basic framework for identifying potential risks, it often falls short in addressing the complexities of modern-day fires. The inclusion of the chemical chain reaction into this model allows for a deeper analysis of ongoing combustion processes, offering insights into how a fire might evolve under different conditions. With this knowledge, firefighting teams can establish more accurate control measures tailored to specific scenarios, significantly improving their response effectiveness.

The importance of this fourth element becomes even more evident when considering the challenges faced in managing and extinguishing fires today. Modern environments introduce a variety of synthetic materials that react differently when burned compared to natural materials. These synthetics often result in hotter, faster-spreading fires, creating additional layers of complexity in fire management. The presence of electric vehicles, lithium-ion batteries, and other advanced technologies introduces new variables into these already complex scenarios. Traditional methods may not suffice to tackle these intricacies, highlighting the necessity of incorporating the fire tetrahedron's principles into our approaches.

Adopting the fire tetrahedron's expanded framework into firefighting strategies leads to significant improvements in tackling blazes. For example, the F-500 Encapsulator Agent (EA) exemplifies how this comprehension translates into practical solutions. Not only does it address fuel, heat, and oxygen, but it also specifically targets the chemical reactions perpetuating the fire. By simultaneously working on all four components, it disrupts the combustion process at multiple levels, demonstrating enhanced efficacy over traditional suppression methods.

Incorporating such advanced tactics means that firefighters can deploy more precise interventions, reducing the time required to bring a fire under control. This results in decreased damage to property and lower risks to human life. Moreover, a well-rounded understanding of the fire tetrahedron fosters innovation in developing new suppression technologies that are more capable of handling the diverse fire scenarios we encounter today.

Moreover, comprehending how these elements interact fundamentally alters firefighting education and training. Personnel are better equipped to assess situations quickly and accurately, plotting out strategies that address each facet of the tetrahedron. This strategic foresight is invaluable in reducing response times and enhancing overall firefighting effectiveness.

Finally, expanding this understanding beyond firefighter training into public awareness can also play a massive role in fire prevention efforts. As communities become more informed about how fires start and spread, they can take proactive measures to mitigate risks within their environments. This collective knowledge empowers individuals and organizations to implement safety measures, from selecting fire-retardant materials in construction to guiding policies that manage land use in fire-prone areas.

Practical Implications for Firefighters

Understanding the foundational elements of fire dynamics, as encapsulated in the fire triangle—comprising heat, fuel, and oxygen—offers significant insights for effective firefighting strategies. Firefighting isn't just about putting out flames; it's about understanding the mechanisms that make fires ignite and propagate. This knowledge is essential for designing effective intervention techniques that help firefighters tackle various types of fires efficiently and safely.

First, identifying and managing each element of the fire triangle is crucial for effective intervention. The fire triangle provides a simplified model that highlights the three essential components needed for a fire to exist. By isolating and controlling one or more of these elements, firefighters can successfully extinguish a blaze. For instance, recognizing the specific fuel source involved in a fire can guide firefighters in determining the best method to remove it or isolate it from other elements of the triangle. Different types of fuels burn at various rates and temperatures, requiring tailored approaches to control or eliminate them (University of South Carolina, 2019). By strategically removing or separating the fuel source, firefighters can effectively limit the fire's ability to sustain itself, thereby aiding in quicker containment.

Moreover, strategies focusing on oxygen reduction serve as powerful methods for suppressing fires by interrupting the combustion process. Oxygen fuels the chemical reactions within a fire; without it, combustion cannot continue (Blazequel, 2024). Techniques like smothering fires with sand or using foam extinguishers work by creating barriers that block oxygen from reaching the flames. In structural firefighting, closing doors and windows can minimize oxygen levels in a burning area, effectively slowing down the fire's spread. Advanced systems such as water mist suppression combine cooling effects with oxygen displacement through steam production, ensuring comprehensive fire suppression by removing multiple sides of the fire triangle simultaneously (Blazequel, 2024). Understanding these techniques empowers firefighters to make informed decisions on the ground, adjusting their tactics according to how oxygen interacts with the other elements involved in a fire scenario.

Controlling heat sources through cooling methods is another practical approach to preventing further ignition and fire growth. Water remains one of the most accessible and effective cooling agents. When applied to fires, water absorbs heat, lowering the temperature of the fuel below its ignition point, which in turn disrupts the combustion process. This technique not only prevents the spread of fire but also helps protect nearby structures and materials from igniting. However, it's essential to recognize situations where water might be ineffective or dangerous, such as with electrical or oil fires, requiring alternative cooling methods or agents (University of South Carolina, 2019). Aerosol agents, for example, are designed to target free radicals and suffocate the fire, while powder agents disperse oxygen away from the fuel.

While each side of the fire triangle plays a distinct role in sustaining a blaze, effective firefighting often involves addressing multiple elements simultaneously. Practical implications for firefighters include developing a clear plan for identifying and controlling each component of the fire triangle in real-world scenarios. This requires an awareness of both the immediate environment and the unique characteristics of the materials involved in the fire. By maintaining situational awareness and adapting techniques to fit the specifics of each incident, firefighters can enhance their effectiveness while minimizing risks to themselves and others.

To aid in this task, it is beneficial to incorporate guidelines for identifying and controlling each component of the fire triangle in practice. This begins with regular training sessions simulating various fire conditions, allowing firefighters to test and refine their skills in managing different elements. Utilizing modern technology, such as thermal imaging cameras, enables firefighters to pinpoint the hottest areas and swiftly direct cooling efforts where they are most needed. Additionally, pre-incident surveys of buildings and landscapes can provide critical information on potential fuel sources and ventilation patterns, offering a strategic advantage when designing fire mitigation plans.

Final Insights

Throughout the chapter, we have delved into the essential and expanded components of fire dynamics, focusing on the foundational elements of the fire triangle—fuel, heat, and oxygen—and their critical role in sustaining a fire. By breaking down each component, we have highlighted how they interact to ignite and propagate fires. Firefighters can effectively mitigate risks by understanding how different types of fuels behave, managing heat sources, and strategically reducing oxygen availability. This knowledge equips them with the ability to make informed decisions quickly, adapting techniques to the specific conditions of an incident.

Furthermore, the introduction of the fire tetrahedron adds depth to our understanding, emphasizing the importance of the chemical chain reaction in maintaining combustion. Recognizing these interactions allows firefighters to anticipate how modern fires might evolve, especially with new challenges presented by synthetic materials and evolving technologies. The integration of this advanced framework into firefighting strategies empowers teams to tackle complex scenarios more precisely and efficiently. As we continue to refine our grasp on these dynamics, both firefighter education and public awareness can play pivotal roles in enhancing safety measures and preventing fire-related incidents in our communities.

Chapter 2 Test Questions and Answers

What are the three components of the fire triangle?

Fuel, heat, and oxygen.

Why is fuel essential in the fire triangle?

Fuel provides the combustible material necessary to sustain a fire.

Give two examples of natural fuels and two examples of synthetic fuels.

Natural fuels: Wood, paper, Synthetic fuels: Gasoline, plastic.

How does the burning behavior of wood differ from gasoline?

Wood burns slowly with a steady flame, while gasoline ignites rapidly with intense heat.

What is a flashover, and how is it related to fuel?

A flashover occurs when all combustible materials in a room reach their ignition temperature simultaneously, resulting in a sudden and intense fire outbreak.

What role does heat play in fire ignition?

Heat acts as the catalyst that elevates the fuel to its ignition temperature, allowing combustion to occur.

List three common sources of heat in fire scenarios.

Open flames, electrical sparks, and friction.

How does heat contribute to fire spread?

Heat spreads through conduction, convection, and radiation, transferring energy to nearby combustible materials and causing them to ignite.

Why is oxygen important in sustaining a fire?

Oxygen supports the chemical reactions within a fire, fueling the combustion process.

What happens when oxygen concentration is reduced during a fire?

Reducing oxygen levels disrupts the combustion process, ultimately extinguishing the fire.

What is the fire tetrahedron, and how does it expand on the fire triangle?

The fire tetrahedron adds a fourth element, the chemical chain reaction, which sustains combustion by generating additional heat.

Why is understanding the chemical chain reaction important for firefighters?

Breaking the chain reaction, using chemical extinguishers or other suppression techniques, can effectively halt a fire's progress.

What modern materials contribute to hotter, faster-spreading fires?

Synthetic materials, electric vehicles, and lithium-ion batteries.

How does the F-500 Encapsulator Agent improve fire suppression?

It targets fuel, heat, oxygen, and the chemical chain reaction simultaneously, effectively disrupting the combustion process.

What techniques are used to reduce oxygen in a fire scenario?

Smothering with sand, using foam extinguishers, and closing doors and windows in structural fires.

How does water function as a cooling agent in fire suppression?

Water absorbs heat, lowering the temperature of the fuel below its ignition point and disrupting the combustion process.

Why might water be ineffective or dangerous in some fire scenarios?

Water may be unsuitable for electrical or oil fires, which require alternative cooling agents like aerosols or powders.

How do thermal imaging cameras assist firefighters?

They help identify the hottest areas, allowing firefighters to target cooling efforts more effectively.

What is one preventive measure that communities can take to reduce fire risks?

Using fire-retardant materials in construction and implementing land-use policies to manage fire-prone areas.

Why is firefighter training essential in managing fire triangle components?

Training helps firefighters simulate various fire conditions, improving their ability to identify and control fuel, heat, and oxygen in real-world scenarios.

Chapter 3: Stages of Fire Development

The stages of fire development are a fundamental concept every firefighter must grasp to effectively respond to and manage fire incidents. Fire evolves through distinct phases, each characterized by unique behaviors and challenges. This understanding is not just about recognizing the flames but dissecting the intricacies behind each stage's progression. Fires begin in an incipient state, growing quietly until they transform into formidable forces. As they evolve, they reach their peak in intensity before eventually decaying. Knowing these stages empowers responders to anticipate how fires develop, which can prove crucial in preventing minor blazes from escalating into catastrophic events.

In this chapter, we delve into the fire's journey, starting with its incipient phase where quick actions can yield significant control. We explore the growth stage, highlighting the perilous transition points that elevate risk levels. The fully developed stage demands a strategic approach due to the intense inferno it represents. Finally, the decay stage is examined for its deceptive calm, underscoring the persistence required to ensure complete extinguishment. Each section delves into key factors influencing these stages—from available fuel types to environmental conditions—offering valuable insights on managing fire dynamics effectively. By understanding these elements, firefighters can make informed decisions, ensuring successful interventions at each critical juncture.

The Four Stages of Fire

Understanding the progression and characteristics of fire stages is essential for firefighters. These stages—Incipient, Growth, Fully Developed, and Decay—each present unique challenges and opportunities for intervention.

The Incipient Stage marks the beginning of a fire when heat, oxygen, and fuel combine to produce ignition. This stage is characterized by small flames and often goes unnoticed until it becomes visible or sets off smoke detectors. Despite its potential for danger, this stage offers optimal conditions for early intervention. At this point, fires can typically be extinguished with minimal resources, such as a handheld fire extinguisher, which can prevent further escalation. Recognizing a fire at this stage is crucial, as quick action can stop its development into a more formidable threat (Chaudhry, 2024).

Moving into the Growth Stage, fire behavior changes significantly. The fire now consumes more fuel and oxygen, leading to increased size and intensity. During this phase, the fire expands rapidly, presenting spatial challenges as it spreads through available combustibles. This is also the stage where flashover may occur—a dangerous situation in which nearly all combustible materials in an enclosed area ignite simultaneously, causing temperatures to soar rapidly, often exceeding 1,000 degrees Fahrenheit (Scheviak, 2021). Flashover signifies a transition point that can overwhelm manual suppression efforts and calls for professional intervention. Understanding these dynamics allows firefighters to anticipate changes in fire behavior and allocate resources effectively.

As the fire transitions to the Fully Developed Stage, it reaches its peak intensity. This stage is marked by maximum heat release and widespread combustion. The fire has consumed most of the available oxygen and fuel, resulting in large flames and thick, black smoke. This phase poses significant dangers to both life and property, with high risks of structural collapse due to intense heat damage. Firefighters face their greatest challenge here, requiring coordinated suppression efforts to combat the extensive blaze. In many cases, this stage demands the use of advanced techniques and equipment to manage the fire's spread and minimize damage (Chaudhry, 2024).

Finally, the Decay Stage occurs as the fire begins to wane. This reduction in activity happens when the fire depletes its supply of fuel or oxygen, leading to a slowdown in combustion. However, the danger is not entirely gone; fires in the decay stage can reignite if additional fuel becomes available. This stage is also associated with risks such as backdraft and smoldering, which can suddenly escalate the situation again. Firefighters must remain vigilant during this phase to prevent re-ignition and ensure that the fire is fully extinguished. Proper ventilation and safe handling techniques are critical in managing this stage efficiently (Scheviak, 2021).

Influencing Factors for Each Stage

In the complex dynamics of fire incidents, understanding the progression of different stages is crucial for effective management and control. One of the primary elements influencing this progression is the type of fuel available. Various materials burn with differing intensities and spread rates, directly impacting how a fire advances. For example, hydrocarbon-based fuels tend to ignite more readily and burn intensely due to their molecular composition, which facilitates easy recombination with oxygen. This can be seen in both structural fires and wildfires where vegetation acts as natural fuel. Larger organic matter like logs takes time to heat up before ignition, whereas smaller twigs or grass catch fire quickly due to their larger surface area relative to mass (Science Learning Hub, 2009). Understanding these differences helps firefighters anticipate fire behavior and tailor control measures accordingly.

Another vital factor is ventilation, which plays a crucial role in supplying oxygen, a necessary element for combustion. Adequate ventilation can increase a fire's intensity by allowing more oxygen to fuel the flames. In contrast, limited ventilation may slow down the process, but it can also lead to dangerous conditions such as backdrafts if oxygen is suddenly reintroduced. Firefighters need to assess building structures or natural barriers that might impede airflow and adjust their strategies to manage the fire's sustainability effectively.

Environmental conditions further influence fire behavior significantly. Weather elements such as wind, temperature, and humidity dictate how fires evolve over time. Wind speeds can dramatically escalate the rate at which fires spread by continuously feeding oxygen and pushing flames toward unburnt areas. Moreover, elevated temperatures and dry weather contribute to lower moisture levels in fuels, making them more susceptible to ignition (UCAR/ COMET, 2024). On the other hand, high humidity or rainfall can dampen vegetation, reducing the likelihood of a fire spreading rapidly. Such environmental insights are essential for predicting changes in fire dynamics through each stage and can guide decisions on resource allocation and firefighting tactics, especially when dealing with large-scale wildfires.

Topography also adds another layer of complexity to the behavior of fires. Steep terrains can preheat fuels through convection and radiation, accelerating the fire's spread uphill. Narrow valleys can channel winds, increasing fire speed and altering its direction unpredictably. Therefore, evaluating the physical landscape is critical in anticipating how a fire might develop and ensuring that firefighters position themselves efficiently to combat the threat.

Recognizing these influencing factors allows for an informed approach when tackling fire incidents. By thoroughly analyzing fuel types, ventilation, and environmental conditions, firefighters can predict potential developments in a fire's trajectory and prepare accordingly. Implementing the right strategies early on can prevent fires from reaching fully developed stages where they consume all available fuels intensely, making suppression efforts more challenging and hazardous. Consequently, this knowledge not only aids in protecting human lives and property but also minimizes ecological damage.

Furthermore, current technological advancements provide tools that assist in monitoring and modeling these variables in real-time. Using satellite data for weather predictions, drones for aerial surveillance, and computer simulations for fire modeling can enhance situational awareness and enable proactive firefighting measures. As a result, firefighters become better equipped to make quick, informed decisions that can alter the course of a fire incident positively.

Predicting Fire Behavior Across Stages

Understanding the progression of fire stages is crucial for effective firefighting. This knowledge provides insights into the potential evolution and severity of incidents, enabling firefighters to anticipate changes and make informed decisions in real-time. Recognizing the different stages of a fire—from incipient to decay—helps in predicting fire behavior, allowing responders to stay one step ahead.

One of the most critical aspects of managing fire incidents is anticipating the transition points between stages. Fires do not progress linearly or predictably; instead, they can accelerate rapidly under certain conditions. For example, the transition from the growth stage to the fully developed stage often signifies a drastic increase in intensity and spread potential. Being able to forecast these shifts means that resources can be allocated more efficiently. Firefighters can assign personnel to strategic locations, prepare equipment tailored to the current and expected conditions, and adjust tactics to mitigate risks effectively.

Recognizing signs of stage shifts is vital for improving situational awareness and tactical planning. A trained firefighter should be vigilant about cues such as smoke color, heat levels, and flame behavior, which indicate changes in fire dynamics. For instance, black, billowing smoke may suggest that a fire is transitioning from the incipient to the growth stage, necessitating immediate intervention to prevent escalation. Incorporating this observational skill into routine assessments enables teams to make tactical adjustments on-the-fly, optimizing their combat strategies under pressure.

Data-driven predictions play an essential role in supporting strategic interventions during firefighting operations. By using models and historical data, incident commanders can better understand how environmental factors like wind direction, humidity, and topography influence fire behavior. These predictions help in formulating actions that minimize damage and enhance safety outcomes. For instance, if data suggests a shift in wind patterns that could exacerbate fire spread towards populated areas, preemptive measures can be taken, such as creating firebreaks or evacuating vulnerable zones.

The OODA Loop, a concept originally developed by military strategist Col. John Boyd, underscores the importance of rapid decision-making in dynamic situations. In the context of fire management, it involves observing the fire's status, orienting oneself with the available information and experience, deciding on the best course of action, and acting decisively (Rielage, 2024). Implementing this iterative process ensures that firefighters remain adaptable, constantly updating their strategies based on the latest observations and predictions. It also emphasizes the importance of continuous learning and adjustment, reinforcing the need for a proactive approach to fire management.

Implementing guidelines can further aid in enhancing decision-making processes. Firefighters should engage in regular training sessions that include simulations of various fire scenarios, emphasizing the identification of transition cues and the importance of adaptive resource allocation. Such exercises allow them to build muscle memory and critical thinking skills required for split-second decisions in high-pressure environments. Additionally, employing technology such as thermal imaging cameras and drones equipped with sensors can provide real-time data on fire temperature and movement, significantly enhancing the ability to predict transitions between stages.

Incorporating these insights and practices into daily operations strengthens the overall capability of firefighting teams. Understanding fire stages not only aids in dealing with current incidents effectively but also builds a knowledge base that can be applied to future scenarios. The ability to foresee potential developments allows responders to maximize the impact of their efforts while ensuring the safety of both personnel and the public.

Insights and Implications

The chapter delves into the intricacies of fire dynamics, emphasizing the importance of understanding each stage—Incipient, Growth, Fully Developed, and Decay. Recognizing these stages allows firefighters to tailor their response strategies effectively, using minimal resources during early intervention opportunities and preparing for more intense actions as fires develop. The transition between these stages is crucial, requiring vigilance and adaptability. By being aware of specific indicators such as smoke characteristics and flame behavior, firefighters can make timely decisions that significantly impact the outcome of fire interventions.

Additionally, the chapter highlights influencing factors that play a pivotal role in predicting and managing fire behavior. Various elements including fuel types, ventilation, environmental conditions, and topography must be considered to anticipate changes in a fire's trajectory. These insights, combined with modern technological tools like drones and computer modeling, equip firefighters with enhanced situational awareness, enabling them to plan and execute effective strategies. Understanding and applying these concepts not only bolsters immediate firefighting efforts but also fortifies long-term readiness in managing future fire incidents.

Chapter 3 Test Questions and Answers

What are the four stages of fire development?

Incipient, Growth, Fully Developed, and Decay.

What characterizes the Incipient Stage of fire?

This is the earliest stage when heat, oxygen, and fuel combine to ignite small flames. It often goes unnoticed but presents the best opportunity for early intervention.

What is the primary intervention method during the Incipient Stage?

Using a handheld fire extinguisher to suppress the fire before it escalates.

What distinguishes the Growth Stage in fire development?

The fire expands rapidly, consuming more oxygen and fuel, potentially leading to flashover.

What is a flashover, and why is it dangerous?

A flashover occurs when all combustible materials ignite simultaneously, creating extreme heat often exceeding 1,000°F.

What strategies can firefighters use to prevent flashover?

Cooling techniques such as applying water to ceilings and walls to reduce heat buildup.

What are common signs that a fire is transitioning into the Fully Developed Stage?

Intense heat, thick black smoke, and flames engulfing the majority of available fuel.

Why is the Fully Developed Stage the most dangerous for firefighters?

It presents the highest heat release rate, increasing the risk of structural collapse and severe injury.

What marks the beginning of the Decay Stage?

The fire's fuel and oxygen supply start to diminish, reducing flame intensity.

What risks persist during the Decay Stage?

The possibility of re-ignition if new oxygen or fuel sources become available.

What role does fuel type play in fire behavior?

Different fuels burn at different intensities and rates, influencing fire spread.

How does ventilation impact fire behavior?

Proper ventilation supplies oxygen that can intensify a fire, while limited airflow may slow the spread but create backdraft risks.

Why is topography important in outdoor fire behavior?

Steep terrains can preheat fuels, accelerating fire spread uphill.

What environmental conditions significantly influence fire spread?

Wind, temperature, and humidity affect how rapidly fires grow and spread.

How can technology help firefighters predict fire behavior?

Tools like thermal imaging cameras, drones, and computer models improve situational awareness and guide strategic decisions.

What is the OODA Loop, and how does it apply to firefighting?

A decision-making model involving Observation, Orientation, Decision, and Action that helps firefighters adapt tactics in dynamic fire conditions.

What observable signs help firefighters predict stage transitions?

Changes in smoke color, heat intensity, and flame movement indicate potential shifts in fire stages.

Why is firefighter training essential for managing fire stages?

Training prepares firefighters to identify cues, allocate resources effectively, and react quickly during transitions.

What safety measures are crucial during the Decay Stage?

Proper ventilation, cooling efforts, and continuous monitoring to prevent rekindling or backdrafts.

How can communities mitigate fire risks in vulnerable areas?

By implementing land-use policies, using fire-resistant materials in construction, and promoting fire prevention education.

Chapter 4: Heat Transfer Mechanisms in Fire

Understanding the mechanisms of heat transfer is crucial in grasping the dynamics of fire, a perilous phenomenon that presents significant challenges on and off the field. Heat transfer not only affects how fires behave but also has a profound impact on firefighting tactics. By examining these mechanisms—conduction, convection, and radiation—we can appreciate their individual roles in shaping the spread of fires and informing strategies to combat them effectively. Each heat transfer mechanism necessitates distinct approaches, emphasizing the importance of thorough knowledge in preventing fire escalation and ensuring safety.

Within this chapter, readers will explore how conduction influences fire movement through solid structures, making certain materials more prone to rapid heat gain and loss. Discussion of convection will highlight its role in circulating heat within an environment, illustrating how this process can accelerate fire growth without direct contact. Through the exploration of radiation, the chapter will reveal how energy moves across distances via electromagnetic waves, affecting objects even when they are not in direct proximity to flames. These insights are pivotal for developing comprehensive firefighting strategies that account for material properties, environmental conditions, and tactical interventions. By correlating theory with practice, this chapter offers valuable perspectives that support effective decision-making in real-world fire scenarios.

Conduction, Convection, and Radiation in Heat Transfer

Heat transfer plays a pivotal role in understanding fire dynamics, particularly when examining the mechanisms of conduction, convection, and radiation. Each method not only influences how fires spread but also bears significant implications on firefighting strategies.

Conduction is the process of heat moving through solid materials, crucial for understanding fire behavior. When one part of a structure becomes heated, molecular vibrations cause energy to travel from that hotter area to a cooler section. This movement of thermal energy occurs most efficiently in materials like metals due to their tightly packed molecules. For firefighters, recognizing materials within a burning building that might conduct heat is essential. For instance, metal beams or structural components can rapidly transfer heat to adjacent areas, potentially leading to unexpected fire spread. Knowing which materials are likely to conduct heat helps in predicting how quickly a fire may move and in implementing tactics to halt its progress, such as cooling those elements directly with water hoses.

Turning to convection, this mechanism describes how heat is transported through fluids—both liquids and gases. In a fire scenario, convection is responsible for the upward movement of hot air and gases, significantly impacting the distribution of heat. As air heats up, it expands and becomes less dense, causing it to rise while cooler, denser air moves downwards, creating a cycle. This cycle can transport heat throughout a space and is often visible in the form of smoke plumes rising in a blaze. Understanding convection currents allows firefighters to anticipate how a fire will behave over time. By observing the smoke's movement, they can predict the potential direction and intensity of a fire's spread. Smoke management systems and proper ventilation techniques can be strategically employed to control these currents, helping to contain the fire or direct it away from valuable assets or escape routes.

Radiation, unlike conduction and convection, does not require a medium to transfer heat; instead, it involves the emission of electromagnetic waves. These waves carry energy that can travel even through a vacuum, making radiation a powerful tool in spreading heat over distances. In the context of firefighting, radiant heat poses a unique challenge. It can ignite materials that are not directly exposed to flames by transferring enough energy to increase their temperature to combustion levels. This phenomenon underscores the importance of maintaining a safe distance from intense fires and implementing protective barriers to block or absorb radiant heat. Firefighters must be equipped with gear designed to shield them from such exposure, reducing the risk of injury and enabling them to approach and manage the fire more effectively.

The implications of these heat transfer mechanisms extend beyond initial firefighting efforts. A deep understanding of how heat behaves can guide the development of building codes, influence the design of fire suppression systems, and enhance training programs for emergency responders. By modeling fire scenarios based on these principles, experts can devise strategies to minimize damage and ensure firefighter safety.

However, it's not just about scientific comprehension—applying this knowledge practically can make the difference in critical situations. Identifying points within a building where conduction might lead to rapid fire spread, using ventilation to manipulate convection currents, or positioning personnel to minimize radiation exposure—all are examples of how theory translates into lifesaving practice. As a result, firefighters armed with a thorough grasp of these concepts find themselves better prepared to tackle the diverse challenges posed by real-world fires.

Impact of Heat Transfer Mechanisms on Fire Dynamics and Tactics

Understanding the different mechanisms of heat transfer is essential in developing effective firefighting strategies. This knowledge can significantly influence how firefighters approach a fire scene, helping them contain and extinguish fires more efficiently while minimizing risks.

First, consider conduction, which involves heat transfer through solid materials. In the context of firefighting, an understanding of conduction allows firefighters to isolate fires by removing or altering conductive pathways. For example, if a fire spreads through metal beams due to their high thermal conductivity, firefighters can disrupt this pathway by cooling the material or applying insulating layers to slow down the heat transfer. This tactic helps limit the spread of fire to adjacent areas, providing more time for containment and reducing potential damage.

Convection, on the other hand, refers to heat transfer through the movement of fluids such as air and water. Recognizing convection patterns is crucial for predicting fire expansion. Hot gases and smoke moving upwards and spreading to cooler areas indicate where the fire is likely to move next. By analyzing these patterns, firefighters can make informed decisions about where to position themselves and their equipment. Proper ventilation strategies are based on this understanding, allowing for controlled airflow that helps dissipate heat, reduce smoke levels, and lower the risk of flashover. Such strategies enhance safety and improve visibility during firefighting operations. Noted expert Jennifer Morningstar highlights the importance of understanding heat transfer in reconstructing fire dynamics, emphasizing its role in determining points of origin (Understanding Heat Transfer: A Guide for Fire Investigators | Warren Forensics, n.d.).

Radiation is another critical aspect of heat transfer that must be considered in firefighting. It involves the transfer of energy through electromagnetic waves, meaning it does not require a medium to travel through. Radiant heat can affect objects and structures at considerable distances from the fire source. Understanding radiation's role enables firefighters to establish defensive zones around a fire active area, thereby protecting structures and personnel from radiant heat exposure. These zones serve as barriers to reduce the threat of heat damage, preventing a small fire from escalating into a larger disaster.

Guidelines play a significant role when considering ventilation's impact on fire growth and behavior. Effective ventilation techniques can control airflow within a structure, mitigating the intensity and speed of combustion by managing oxygen availability. Conversely, poor ventilation increases the risk of sudden events like flashovers or backdrafts. Flashover occurs when built-up heat causes all combustible materials in a room to ignite simultaneously, while backdraft results from introducing oxygen to a smoldering environment, causing explosive combustion. Thus, understanding ventilation and heat transfer is imperative for safer firefighting operations (Unlocking the Secrets of Fire Behavior: A Vital Evolution in Firefighting Tactics, 2024).

Both conduction and convection have specific implications for firefighter safety and operational efficiency. Conductive heat transfer can lead to unexpected hot spots and structural weaknesses that pose hazards in a fire environment. Recognizing these dangers requires vigilant observation and timely intervention to prevent accidents. Convection also affects the distribution of products of combustion, such as smoke and toxic gases, complicating efforts to maintain breathable air quality in affected areas. Addressing these challenges demands careful planning and execution, guided by a comprehensive understanding of heat transfer dynamics.

Finally, the effective application of knowledge about radiation extends beyond establishing protective zones. It includes using specialized equipment like thermal imaging cameras to detect heat sources hidden within walls or beneath surfaces. This technology aids in identifying potential rekindles or concealed fires, allowing for prompt action before they escalate. Additionally, it supports tactical decision-making regarding resource allocation and strategic positioning during firefighting efforts.

Ventilation and Fire Spread Dynamics

In firefighting, effective ventilation is a crucial strategy that significantly influences fire growth, flashover risks, and backdraft hazards. Understanding how ventilation impacts these phenomena helps firefighters develop safer and more efficient tactics for controlling fires. When properly managed, ventilation facilitates controlled airflow, which reduces positive pressure within a structure. This reduction in pressure decreases the intensity and speed of fire growth. By introducing a systematic method of allowing smoke and heat to escape, ventilators can decrease the temperature within a burning building, providing a more manageable environment for firefighters and reducing the risk of catastrophic events.

When a fire occurs inside a structure, the accumulation of heat and smoke can create dangerous conditions. Without adequate ventilation, heat builds up rapidly, increasing the risk of a flashover. Flashovers occur when accumulated heat reaches such a high level that all combustible materials in a confined space ignite almost simultaneously. This transition from a developing to a fully developed fire presents significant danger to occupants and responders. Indicators such as rapid flame spread or glazing failures signal impending flashover, highlighting the essential role of timely ventilation in preventing such outcomes. Flashover is a testament to the importance of understanding thermal dynamics in firefighting, emphasizing the need for precise control over airflow to prevent its occurrence (Drysdale, 1998).

On the other hand, backdrafts pose another serious threat during firefighting operations. A backdraft happens when a smoldering fire, deprived of sufficient oxygen, suddenly receives fresh air. This introduction of oxygen leads to rapid combustion and often results in an explosive burst. The dangers of backdrafts lie not only in their suddenness but also in their capacity to cause structural damage and put firefighter lives at risk. Recognizing environments prone to backdraft is essential, as is using ventilation strategies that either mitigate or avert them entirely. In scenarios where a fire is ventilation-controlled, it's critical to introduce fresh air carefully. Increasing ventilation too quickly can cause a dangerous increase in the rate of heat release, potentially leading to a backdraft (Grimwood et al., 2005; Karlsson & Quintiere, 2000).

In practical terms, managing ventilation involves a delicate balance. Firefighters must assess fire growth patterns and respond accordingly, using tools like thermal imaging cameras to evaluate temperature changes and smoke movement. When possible, they should employ mechanical ventilation techniques to ensure a steady and controlled release of heat and toxic gases without inadvertently feeding the fire with excess oxygen. Identifying the right moment to ventilate and choosing the appropriate method are skills honed through training and experience, underscoring their criticality in fireground operations.

Effective ventilation serves as a double-edged sword by dispersing hot gases while preventing overheated conditions that facilitate flashover. However, introducing fresh air too liberally can exacerbate the fire, transforming a containable situation into a major conflagration. Therefore, it's vital that ventilation efforts are precisely coordinated and executed. Doing so involves evaluating the fire's stage and the structural layout, as well as understanding the behavior of smoke and heat inside the building. This advanced knowledge equips firefighters to make informed decisions about vent points and manage internal temperatures effectively.

In addition to controlling fire growth, ventilation provides a tactical advantage by improving visibility and access for rescue operations, further enhancing firefighter safety and effectiveness. Removing smoke and heated gases clears pathways, allowing teams to perform rescues, advance hoselines, and efficiently extinguish the fire. Firefighters must navigate the complexities of each unique incident, considering factors such as wind direction, building configuration, and existing fire dynamics to optimize ventilation plans.

Training is key in learning how to leverage ventilation to prevent flashover and avoid backdraft. Frequent drills focusing on ventilation scenarios allow firefighters to better understand how these phenomena manifest in real-world situations. Simulations using controlled burns help crews recognize symptoms indicating the approach of a flashover or the potential for a backdraft, positioning them to act swiftly and decisively. These educational programs emphasize both theoretical concepts and practical applications, fortifying the knowledge necessary to conduct safe and successful operations.

Overall, mastering ventilation techniques is an integral aspect of modern firefighting. By reducing the probability of flashover and mitigating backdraft risks, firefighters can better protect themselves and those they serve. Ventilation's ability to shape fire behavior underscores its place as a cornerstone of fire dynamics education. As new technologies and methodologies emerge, continuous learning and adaptation are essential to maintain the efficacy of these life-saving strategies.

Final Analysis

Understanding the mechanisms of heat transfer—conduction, convection, and radiation—is a fundamental aspect of developing effective firefighting tactics. By grasping how these processes impact fire behavior, firefighters can better anticipate the challenges posed by different fire scenarios. Conduction highlights the need to recognize materials within a structure that might facilitate the unexpected spread of fire, while convection underlines the importance of monitoring airflow and smoke patterns to predict the fire's path. Radiation emphasizes maintaining safe distances and implementing protective strategies to shield against intense heat.

These insights extend well beyond immediate firefighting efforts, influencing building design and emergency planning. Knowledge of heat transfer allows firefighters to make informed decisions about how to isolate fires, manage ventilation, and create defensive zones, ultimately enhancing their ability to protect lives and property. With this understanding, firefighters improve their operational effectiveness and safety, ensuring they are better prepared to tackle the diverse challenges faced in real-world fire incidents.

Chapter 4 Test Questions and Answers

What are the three primary mechanisms of heat transfer in fire dynamics?

Conduction, convection, and radiation.

Why is understanding heat transfer crucial for firefighting tactics?

It helps predict fire spread, develop effective strategies, and ensure firefighter safety.

How can knowledge of heat transfer influence building codes and fire suppression systems?

It guides material selection, structural design, and ventilation planning to minimize fire risks.

What is conduction in the context of fire behavior?

Conduction is the transfer of heat through solid materials by molecular vibrations.

Why are metal beams particularly concerning during a fire?

Metal conducts heat efficiently, potentially spreading fire to adjacent areas rapidly.

What tactic can firefighters use to reduce fire spread via conduction?

Cooling heated materials directly with water or applying insulating layers.

What is convection in fire dynamics?

Convection is the transfer of heat through fluids, such as air and smoke.

How does convection contribute to fire spread?

Rising hot air carries heat upward, spreading fire to upper floors and distant areas.

What visual indicator can help firefighters predict fire movement through convection?

Observing the movement and behavior of smoke plumes.

How can ventilation be used to manage convection during firefighting?

Proper ventilation controls airflow, dissipates heat, and reduces the risk of flashover.

What distinguishes radiation from conduction and convection?

Radiation transfers heat via electromagnetic waves and does not require a medium.

How can radiant heat ignite materials without direct flame contact?

Radiant energy increases temperatures enough to reach combustion levels.

What protective measures can firefighters take against radiant heat?

Establish defensive zones and wear heat-resistant protective gear.

How can firefighters use conduction knowledge to contain fires?

By identifying and cooling conductive materials to slow fire spread.

What is a common method to control convection-driven fire growth?

Creating ventilation points to channel smoke and heat away from critical areas.

Why is radiation a major concern even for distant objects?

Radiant energy can transfer enough heat to ignite materials from afar.

What is a flashover?

A dangerous event where accumulated heat causes all combustible materials in a room to ignite simultaneously.

What are common indicators that a flashover may occur?

Rapid flame spread, glazing of windows, or increasing heat intensity.

What is a backdraft?

A sudden explosion occurs when fresh air is introduced to a smoldering fire.

How can firefighters minimize the risk of backdraft during ventilation?

By introducing fresh air slowly and in controlled amounts to prevent sudden combustion.

Chapter 5: Fire Spread and Propagation

Understanding fire spread and propagation is fundamental in the field of firefighting. Fire spread describes how fires move across landscapes, structures, or any medium that facilitates combustion, creating scenarios that can quickly escalate in intensity. Those dedicated to firefighting must understand these dynamics to effectively combat and prevent uncontrolled fires. As fires move, they are influenced by a myriad of elements that interact at different levels, making fire behavior a complex subject requiring comprehensive analysis.

This chapter delves into several critical aspects of fire spread, exploring factors such as fuel types, weather conditions, and terrain that significantly influence fire movement. It outlines how these elements shape both horizontal and vertical fire propagation, detailing their roles in determining the speed and trajectory of fire spread. Additionally, the chapter addresses the intricacies of fire spread in varying environments—from open fields subject to wind dynamics to multi-story buildings where vertical spread poses unique challenges. Through this exploration, readers will gain insights into essential techniques and strategies for predicting and managing fire behavior, ultimately serving as a crucial foundation for firefighting practices and improving readiness in the face of potential fire threats.

Factors That Influence Fire Spread

Understanding the elements that influence fire spread is critical for firefighters and land managers aiming to effectively manage and combat wildfires. Key factors such as fuel types, weather conditions, and terrain play pivotal roles in the dynamics of fire behavior. By examining these components, we can develop a clearer picture of how fires propagate across various environments.

One of the primary drivers that affect fire spread is the type and arrangement of fuels in the fire's path. Fuels can be anything from grasses to dense forests, each burning at different rates and intensities. For instance, fine fuels like dry grasses ignite quickly and burn with rapid speed, potentially spreading a fire faster than heavier fuels like logs or stumps, which require more energy to ignite but sustain burning longer once they catch fire (Loudermilk et al., 2022). Understanding the characteristics of these fuels enables fire practitioners to predict fire behavior in different ecological settings and adjust their strategies accordingly. As noted by Archibald et al. (2018), recognizing vegetation as more than just fuel allows us to integrate its ecological role, impacting fire dynamics significantly.

Weather conditions are another crucial factor modifying fire behavior. Wind, humidity, and temperature all interact to determine the intensity and direction of a fire. High winds can increase the rate at which a fire spreads by carrying embers over large distances, sometimes kilometers ahead of the main fire front. Meanwhile, low humidity levels can dry out potential fuels, making them more prone to ignition and quicker to burn. Conversely, high humidity often dampens fuels and slows fire progress. Temperature also plays a role; higher temperatures can preheat fuels, lowering their ignition threshold and potentially quickening fire spread (admin, 2024).

Terrain and topography, including slopes and elevation, significantly influence the movement patterns of fires. Fires generally move more rapidly uphill than downhill due to the convective heat rising from flames preheating the upper slope fuels, thus enhancing combustion (admin, 2024). Steeper slopes amplify this effect, causing fires to accelerate even further. Furthermore, topographical features like valleys and ridges can act as natural barriers or paths for fire movement, altering wind patterns and thereby affecting how and where a fire spreads.

A comprehensive understanding of these factors not only helps in predicting fire behavior but also aids in designing effective firefighting strategies and mitigating potential damage. This knowledge supports efforts in prescribed burning, where controlled fires are used to reduce fuel loads and prevent larger wildfires. By considering fuel types, weather, and terrain, land managers can create safer and more predictable outcomes for both ecological management and fire suppression activities (Hiers et al., 2020).

Horizontal and Vertical Spread

Fire spread across surfaces and through structures is a complex process influenced by numerous factors. Understanding these mechanisms is vital for firefighters who wish to deepen their knowledge of fire dynamics. Fire can propagate horizontally and vertically, each with unique characteristics and challenges.

Horizontal fire spread involves flames moving across flat surfaces such as floors or open fields. This type of spread is primarily affected by the continuity of combustible materials. For instance, a wooden floor provides an uninterrupted path for fire to advance, unlike a metal floor, which acts as a barrier due to its non-combustible nature. Wind plays a significant role in horizontal fire spread as well. When a strong breeze blows across a field of dry grass, it acts like a bellows, fanning the flames and promoting rapid propagation. Conversely, in a sheltered environment where wind exposure is minimized, horizontal spread may be slower and more contained.

In contrast, vertical fire spread presents different challenges. This involves the upward movement of flames through buildings and other multi-story structures. The tendency for heat to rise—known as buoyancy—is a key driver. Flames naturally extend upwards, taking advantage of natural ventilation paths such as stairwells, elevator shafts, and unsealed gaps in construction, which act like chimneys (Williams, 1977). These features allow hot gases and flames to travel swiftly from one floor to the next, exacerbating the spread of fire. It is crucial for firefighters to recognize these pathways to effectively mitigate the vertical spread.

Multi-story buildings present additional complexities for fire spread due to their diverse construction materials and designs. Each building is unique, with variations in structural layout, materials used, and the integration of fire-resistant technologies. For example, modern buildings often use glass panels or aluminum cladding, which can fail under intense heat, allowing fire access to upper floors (Ashenhurst, 2018). Furthermore, gaps in insulation or protective barriers can serve as conduits for flames, making it easier for fires to leap from one story to another. It's essential to understand how these design elements influence fire behavior to devise effective firefighting strategies.

As part of understanding the vertical spread, the concept of the "chimney effect" must be considered. In structures designed with open atriums or connected spaces, this phenomenon becomes particularly pronounced. As hot air rises, it creates a draft that draws cooler air from lower levels, feeding the flames with a continuous supply of oxygen. This not only accelerates the fire's upward movement but also poses additional risks, such as increased smoke production and heightened temperatures on upper floors, which can hinder evacuation efforts and create hazardous conditions for inhabitants and first responders.

Effective fire containment relies on identifying potential weak points within a structure. Areas where fire-resistant materials are lacking or where gaps between fire barriers exist are especially vulnerable. For instance, curtain wall systems—used in many high-rise buildings for their aesthetic appeal and energy efficiency—can become liabilities in a fire event if their design does not adequately address potential spread through window transoms or perimeter voids (Ashenhurst, 2018). Therefore, regular inspections and maintenance of these areas are critical to ensure they meet safety standards.

Additionally, the interaction between different materials during a fire must be understood. Some materials are inherently flame-retardant, while others require treatment or additional protection to resist ignition. For example, concrete and steel structures are typically more resistant to fire compared to wood or plastic-based components. However, when exposed to prolonged heat, even these robust materials can suffer structural degradation, necessitating comprehensive fire-resistant coatings or insulative barriers to preserve their integrity.

The principles of fire spread highlight the importance of designing and maintaining buildings with proactive fire safety measures. Building codes and regulations often dictate the minimum requirements for fire resistance, but going beyond these basics can provide better protection. Installing automatic sprinkler systems, ensuring proper sealing of joints and penetrations, and employing compartmentalization techniques are all proven methods to slow down or prevent the spread of fire, granting occupants more time to escape and firefighters greater opportunity to control the blaze before it intensifies.

Understanding fire propagation is not solely about recognizing the threat; it's also about implementing effective prevention strategies. Regular training and simulations for firefighters can greatly improve their ability to anticipate fire behavior, adapt to rapidly changing conditions, and make informed decisions during an emergency. Knowledge of fire dynamics empowers them to identify critical intervention points, enhancing overall operational efficiency and safety.

Firefighting Preparation: Knowledge and Skills

In the realm of firefighting, possessing essential knowledge and skills is pivotal for effectively combating fires. These skills not only save lives but also protect properties and ecosystems from potentially devastating impacts. Pre-incident planning stands at the forefront of these competencies. It involves a proactive approach to fire management by predicting fire behavior, identifying potential hazards, and understanding building construction.

Predicting fire behavior is essential for anticipating how a fire might spread under various conditions. This requires an understanding of fire behavior prediction models, which help in estimating the speed and direction of fire spread. Firefighters use data from past fire incidents, weather conditions, and terrain analysis to forecast fire trajectories. Implementing these models effectively can be the difference between timely intervention and uncontrolled fire escalation. (*Fire Safety Training: A Comprehensive Guide*, n.d.)

Identifying potential hazards within response areas is another crucial aspect of pre-incident planning. This involves recognizing flammable materials, fuel loads, and possible ignition sources that could exacerbate fire situations. By conducting thorough assessments of response areas, firefighters can create strategic plans that address these hazards before they become active threats.

Understanding building construction and materials is vital, particularly when dealing with urban fires. Different building materials behave differently under fire conditions, affecting fire spread and structural integrity. Firefighting teams need to familiarize themselves with the construction types prevalent in their jurisdictions to predict potential collapse points and access routes during operations.

Comprehensive training is the backbone of firefighting readiness. A well-rounded training program includes learning fire behavior principles through theoretical knowledge and practical drills. Simulations play a significant role here, offering a controlled environment for firefighters to experience realistic scenarios. These exercises enhance their ability to make quick decisions, adapt to changing conditions, and execute effective intervention strategies. In particular, scenario-based exercises focused on confined spaces, high-rise buildings, and wildfire settings prepare firefighters for diverse challenges. (*Courses | National Advanced Fire & Resource Institute*, 2024)

Familiarity with different fuel types and their properties is another critical component of firefighter training. Understanding the combustion characteristics of materials such as wood, plastics, and chemicals enables firefighters to choose appropriate suppression tactics. For instance, some fuels may require water-based extinguishers, while others necessitate foam or dry chemical agents.

Training in reading smoke and fire conditions is equally imperative. Smoke patterns provide valuable insights into the fire's location, intensity, and the type of materials burning. By interpreting smoke signals, firefighters can assess ventilation paths and predict potential fire spread, allowing them to position themselves strategically and avoid hazardous zones.

Firefighter awareness of environmental conditions is a skill that comes into play during actual firefighting operations. Recognizing changes in weather, such as wind shifts, humidity levels, and temperature fluctuations, is essential for adapting firefighting techniques in real-time. For example, increased wind speeds can accelerate wildfire spread, requiring adjustments in containment strategies. (*Fire Safety Training: A Comprehensive Guide*, n.d.)

Monitoring fuel load variances in wildland fires is an area where situational awareness proves vital. Fuel loads refer to the amount of combustible material present in an area, which directly influences fire intensity and propagation speed. Firefighters must continually assess these variances to predict how a fire will behave and deploy resources accordingly.

Understanding smoke patterns and behaviors further enhances firefighter safety and effectiveness. Observing how smoke moves through different environments provides clues about the underlying fire dynamics. Sudden changes in smoke color or density can signal impending danger, highlighting the importance of vigilance and timely decision-making during operations.

Observing building materials and structural integrity during fire events is another key aspect of firefighter awareness. Buildings made of steel, wood, or concrete react differently to heat, potentially leading to partial or total collapses. Being aware of these construction nuances helps firefighters develop safer approaches to entering buildings and conducting rescue operations.

Final Thoughts

This chapter has thoroughly examined the numerous elements that influence the dynamics of fire spread. Understanding these factors is essential for firefighters, who regularly face unpredictable conditions in their line of duty. By investigating how fuel types, weather, and terrain interact to affect fire behavior, this analysis equips fire professionals with the knowledge necessary to anticipate potential fire movements. Recognizing that various fuels burn differently helps in predicting how fires will progress through diverse environments. Additionally, insight into how weather conditions like wind and humidity can alter a fire's path or intensity aids in adjusting strategies accordingly. Terrain also plays a significant role, as the landscape can either hinder or accelerate fire spread, impacting firefighting efforts.

Building on this foundational understanding, the discussion advances into exploring horizontal and vertical fire spreads, emphasizing the challenges faced within different settings. The mechanics of fire propagation through structures highlight the need for awareness of building materials and construction design. Knowing how materials respond to heat allows for better strategizing during operations. Furthermore, recognizing patterns such as the "chimney effect" in multi-story buildings underscores the importance of identifying potential weaknesses that could exacerbate fire spread. Through effective training and pre-incident planning based on these dynamics, firefighters can enhance their ability to predict dangerous developments and execute timely, informed interventions. This comprehensive approach ensures not only the safety of firefighters but also the protection of communities and ecosystems they serve.

Chapter 5 Test Questions and Answers

What is fire spread?

Fire spread describes how fires move across landscapes, structures, or any medium that facilitates combustion, often escalating in intensity.

Why is understanding fire spread important for firefighters?

Understanding fire spread helps firefighters predict fire behavior, implement effective strategies, and mitigate potential damage.

What are the three key factors that influence fire spread?

Fuel types, weather conditions, and terrain.

How do fine fuels like dry grasses impact fire spread?

Fine fuels ignite quickly and burn rapidly, accelerating fire spread.

How do heavier fuels like logs or stumps behave in a fire?

They require more energy to ignite but sustain burning longer once ignited.

How does wind affect fire behavior?

Wind increases fire spread by carrying embers over long distances and intensifying flame movement.

What role does humidity play in fire behavior?

Low humidity dries out fuels, increasing their flammability, while high humidity dampens fuels and slows fire spread.

How does temperature influence fire spread?

Higher temperatures preheat fuels, lowering their ignition threshold and accelerating fire growth.

Why do fires move faster uphill than downhill?

Rising heat preheats fuels above the fire, accelerating combustion on slopes.

What are some terrain features that can alter fire movement?

Valleys, ridges, and slopes can act as natural barriers or conduits for fire spread.

Why is pre-incident planning important for firefighters?

It helps predict fire behavior, identify hazards, and develop effective intervention strategies.

What is the value of understanding building materials for firefighters?

Knowing how different materials respond to heat helps firefighters anticipate structural failures and choose safer entry points.

Chapter 6: Ventilation and Fire Dynamics

Ventilation is a vital component in understanding fire dynamics and ensuring safe firefighting practices. It acts as both an ally and a potential adversary, influencing how fires grow and behave within various environments. The intricate relationship between ventilation and fire behavior demands a comprehensive understanding to effectively manage fire incidents. Firefighters face numerous challenges, including managing air flow, adapting to changing conditions, and making real-time decisions that could significantly impact the outcome of a fire situation. By acknowledging the critical role of ventilation, personnel involved in fire management can enhance their strategies, focusing on identifying optimal ventilation approaches to protect lives and property.

This chapter delves into crucial concepts that form the foundation of effective firefighting strategies. Key topics include an exploration of both positive and negative ventilation methods, highlighting their implications on fire growth and smoke movement. Readers will gain insights into phenomena such as flashover and backdraft, learning how these events relate to ventilation practices. The text further emphasizes situational awareness and decision-making under pressure, underscoring the importance of training and preparedness. Through case studies and historical examples, we examine the consequences of mismanaged ventilation, aiming to equip firefighters with essential knowledge for safer operations. Analyzing ventilation-influenced scenarios provides practical guidance on enhancing operational effectiveness while minimizing risks during firefighting efforts.

Ventilation's Influence on Fire Behavior

Ventilation plays a pivotal role in the dynamics of fire behavior, impacting everything from growth and spread to smoke movement within a structure. Firefighters must understand how ventilation affects fire dynamics to ensure effective firefighting strategies and safety. At the heart of this understanding are concepts like positive and negative ventilation, flashover, backdraft, and how ventilation influences these phenomena.

Positive ventilation involves introducing air into a fire environment to support combustion. It can be beneficial in certain situations, such as when firefighters need to clear smoke quickly or when they aim to direct fire spread away from specific areas. However, it's essential to apply this strategy with caution since adding oxygen can increase a fire's intensity if not managed properly. On the other hand, negative ventilation aims to remove air from the fire scene, typically by using exhaust fans or creating exit points for smoke and heat. This approach can help control a fire by limiting the available oxygen—a crucial factor in slowing down combustion and reducing fire intensity. Understanding the differences between these types of ventilation is fundamental for firefighters to choose the appropriate method depending on the situation they face.

When considering how ventilation impacts fire growth and spread, one must recognize how it alters the fire environment. Ventilation changes can rapidly transform a smoldering fire into a fully developed blaze. Introducing more air often means providing the fire with additional fuel (oxygen), leading to faster growth and spreading through connected spaces. Fire can quickly propagate through open paths, especially in structures that include interconnected compartments with minimal barriers. Furthermore, smoke movement is significantly influenced by ventilation. As fresh air enters, smoke and hot gases travel towards the exhaust points, allowing firefighters to observe the fire's path, adapt their tactics, and prevent entrapment.

Flashover represents a critical phase in fire development where all combustible materials in an area ignite almost simultaneously due to extremely high temperatures and accumulated flammable gases. This occurrence marks the transition from a growing fire to a fully developed fire, presenting significant danger to both occupants and firefighters. The key to preventing flashover lies in effective ventilation management—regulating the introduction of air and controlling temperatures can delay or even prevent this rapid escalation. Ventilation-induced flashover highlights the need for cautious planning, as providing too much air could accelerate the heat release rate and lead to catastrophic results.

Conversely, backdraft refers to the sudden ignition of combustible gases when a new air source is introduced to an oxygen-starved environment filled with trapped gases. Backdrafts are particularly dangerous as they occur without warning and can cause explosive reactions. While flashovers develop over time, backdrafts happen when enclosed spaces receive a sudden influx of oxygen. Firefighters need to identify potential backdraft conditions, recognizing signs such as yellowish smoke or tightly sealed windows, before implementing any ventilation method.

To mitigate the risks associated with flashover and backdraft, strategic ventilation plans should incorporate various safety protocols. Firefighters must assess the burning regime—whether the fire is fuel-controlled or ventilation-controlled—and make informed decisions based on observed conditions and potential hazards. During a ventilation-controlled burn, the fire's intensity depends primarily on oxygen availability, making controlled ventilation intervention vital. Effective execution requires coordination between ventilation teams and those involved in attacking the fire directly, ensuring that air supply and heat exhaustion align.

Moreover, the impact of tactical ventilation on fire dynamics relies heavily on real-time decision-making and situational awareness. In high-pressure environments, evaluating variables like wind direction, building configuration, compartmentalization, and presence of openings is critical to formulating safe approaches. Horizontal ventilation, for instance, might provide quick improvements by raising hot gas layers, but if uncoordinated, it can escalate fire conditions harmful to personnel.

Historically, unfortunate incidents have showcased the dire consequences of mismanaged ventilation, emphasizing the importance of comprehensive training and continuous learning among firefighters. Proper education equips them with the necessary skills to interpret visual cues, learn from case studies, and implement best practices during actual operations. By honing their capability to predict potential outcomes of various ventilation strategies, firefighters enhance their effectiveness and safeguard lives.

Behavior of Ventilation-Controlled Fires

Ventilation-controlled fires are a critical aspect of modern firefighting dynamics. These types of fires occur when the development and behavior of the fire are significantly influenced by the availability of oxygen rather than the amount of fuel present. This distinction is crucial as it shapes how fires behave under different ventilation conditions, impacting both the intensity and the potential spread.

When ventilation is restricted, fires tend to exhibit slower growth due to limited oxygen supply. In these conditions, the combustion process is hampered, which may initially appear to work in favor of containment efforts. However, this creates a volatile environment where any sudden introduction of air can trigger rapid intensification. The moment a window breaks or a door is opened, oxygen floods the confined space, leading to a potential surge in heat release and fire growth. This effect underscores why understanding the balance between fuel and air is imperative for firefighters managing such scenarios. On the other hand, when ventilation is maximized, either intentionally or accidentally, the ample oxygen supply fuels the fire more vigorously, resulting in faster spread and increased temperatures. Recognizing these dynamics assists firefighters in predicting fire behavior under various circumstances to strategically plan their interventions.

Developing effective firefighter strategies for managing ventilation at different fire scenarios is paramount for controlling fire spread and ensuring safety. One successful approach involves coordinating tactical ventilation with suppression efforts. For instance, before initiating ventilation procedures, attack lines must be positioned and ready to deliver water directly onto the main body of the fire. This coordination minimizes the risk of escalating fire intensity, an essential consideration highlighted in past incidents where premature ventilation led to adverse outcomes. Moreover, employing techniques such as creating controlled openings away from the current fire location helps channel smoke and heat while preventing the fire from reaching unburned areas quickly. When executed properly, these strategies can efficiently regulate fire progression within structures.

A key component of effective ventilation management is situational awareness combined with real-time decision-making. Firefighting operations are dynamic, demanding constant adaptation to evolving conditions on the ground. Utilizing information such as changing smoke colors, the speed of flame spread, and the structure's layout enables informed decisions regarding ventilation tactics. For example, monitoring smoke movement patterns can provide insights into the fire's locations and potential weak points within the structure. Additionally, advanced technology like thermal imaging cameras offers firefighters the ability to see through dense smoke, identifying hotspots that require additional focus. This comprehensive awareness serves as the foundation for evaluating when and where to adjust ventilation actions to optimize impact and prevent surprises that could compromise operational safety.

Adjusting ventilation during firefighting operations presents inherent risks and challenges. One major risk involves backdraft, a dangerous phenomenon where a sudden influx of oxygen into an oxygen-depleted area results in explosive ignition of combustible gases. To mitigate this, firefighters must exercise discipline in timing their ventilation actions—particularly delaying ventilations until suppression lines are set and actively working. Moreover, misinterpreting structural indicators could lead to unintended consequences, such as unintentionally enhancing the fire's energy release or compromising escape routes. Training and experience are invaluable assets in honing intuition and sharpening judgment to address these complexities. Through rigorous scenario-based training and drills, firefighters simulate various ventilation-limited situations, fostering familiarity and proficiency in handling unexpected challenges effectively.

To support these principles, guidelines can enhance operational success. For ventilation-controlled fires, implementing clear protocols ensures consistency and efficacy under pressure. Guidelines should specify when tactical venting should commence, who directs it, and how communication flows among team members. Practicing vent discipline is crucial; awareness of the negative impact random venting may cause serves as a reminder of the importance of timing, sequence, and prior suppression readiness. By incorporating these guidelines, firefighting operations benefit from structured yet adaptable approaches tailored to diverse fire environments.

Smoke and Gas Movement Analysis

Understanding smoke movement patterns is crucial for predicting fire behavior and ensuring effective firefighting strategies. Smoke forms when materials combust, releasing a variety of gases that can be hazardous to both firefighters and occupants. Toxic gases like carbon monoxide (CO) and carbon dioxide $(CO2)$, among others, are produced during combustion and pose significant risks. These gases can reduce oxygen levels and impair breathing, highlighting the importance of understanding their formation and impact. Recognizing these dangers allows firefighters to take necessary precautions when entering environments saturated with smoke and gas.

The behavior of smoke varies greatly depending on whether it is contained within an enclosed space or allowed to disperse in open areas. In confined spaces, smoke and heat accumulate rapidly, creating dangerous conditions and potentially leading to phenomena like flashover. The temperature of the environment, ventilation paths, and building layouts all influence how smoke moves. For example, in a high-rise building, smoke might travel vertically through stairwells more swiftly, posing challenges for evacuation and rescue operations. Conversely, in an open setting, smoke disperses faster but could obscure visibility over a wide area. Understanding these differences is vital for strategic planning and executing safe operations.

Analyzing smoke patterns serves as a critical skill for tactical decision-making during firefighting efforts. Firefighters must be adept at reading the visual cues presented by smoke—its color, thickness, and speed can offer valuable insights into the fire's location, intensity, and potential spread. Darker, thicker smoke suggests incomplete combustion and indicates a lack of oxygen, while lighter-colored smoke may mean more complete combustion with different fuel characteristics. Furthermore, the speed at which smoke moves could imply varying pressure zones within a structure, helping predict how a fire might evolve if unchecked.

Comprehensive training programs play an essential role in equipping firefighters with the skills necessary to recognize and interpret smoke signals effectively. This training often involves simulations and controlled burns, where firefighters can hone their abilities to anticipate fire developments based on smoke behavior. Such exercises allow them to practice forming strategies that prioritize safety and effectiveness, reducing the risk to themselves and potential victims.

Utilizing these skills in real-time scenarios can significantly enhance overall fireground strategy. By observing the smoke's behavior, firefighters can make informed decisions on ventilation tactics, entry points, and fire attack methods. This strategic use of information ensures that operations are not only efficient but also safer for all involved. For example, knowing when to ventilate a building can prevent situations where introducing fresh air could exacerbate the fire's intensity or lead to backdraft conditions.

Guidelines for analyzing smoke patterns are particularly valuable in advancing tactical decision-making. When evaluating smoke, consider its origin — is it coming from a specific room or spreading throughout a structure? Monitoring changes over time can indicate shifts in fire dynamics, providing clues to possible flashover or backdraft scenarios. Furthermore, collaboration among team members to share observations enhances situational awareness, allowing for rapid adaptation to evolving conditions.

Lessons Learned

In this chapter, we explored the intricate relationship between ventilation and fire behavior. Understanding how different types of ventilation—positive and negative—impact fire dynamics is crucial for developing effective firefighting strategies. Ventilation can either accelerate a fire's growth or help in controlling it by managing the available oxygen. By recognizing the potential for phenomena such as flashover and backdraft, firefighters can better assess risks and adapt their tactics accordingly. Emphasizing the importance of strategic ventilation planning and coordination ensures that air supply and heat exhaustion align effectively with suppression efforts, minimizing the dangers involved.

The analysis of smoke movement plays a significant role in predicting fire behavior and determining the proper tactical responses. Learning to interpret smoke signals can provide insights into the fire's intensity and spread, enabling informed decision-making on ventilation methods and attack strategies. This chapter stressed the importance of situational awareness and real-time decision-making to evaluate variables like wind direction and compartmentalization, enhancing operational success. By honing these skills through comprehensive training, firefighters can increase their effectiveness and ensure safety during challenging scenarios. Through vigilance and well-informed actions, they can optimize their response to fires under various conditions, ultimately safeguarding lives and property.

Chapter 6 Test Questions and Answers

Why is ventilation considered both an ally and a potential adversary in firefighting?

Ventilation can help control smoke movement and improve visibility, but if mismanaged, it can accelerate fire growth by introducing more oxygen.

What is positive ventilation and when is it used?

Positive ventilation introduces air into the fire environment, often using fans to clear smoke or push fire away from critical areas.

What is negative ventilation and how does it work?

Negative ventilation removes air from a fire scene, typically by creating exhaust points for smoke and heat, reducing available oxygen to the fire.

How can improper ventilation increase fire intensity?

Introducing excessive oxygen can feed the fire, causing it to spread faster and burn more intensely.

What is flashover and why is it dangerous?

Flashover occurs when all combustible materials in a room ignite simultaneously, marking the transition to a fully developed fire with extreme temperatures.

How does ventilation influence the likelihood of a flashover?

Ventilation can accelerate flashover by introducing oxygen, increasing heat release, and promoting rapid fire growth.

What are the warning signs of an impending flashover?

Indicators include intense heat, rapid smoke movement, and visible flames rolling across the ceiling.

What is a backdraft and how does it differ from flashover?

A backdraft occurs when oxygen is suddenly introduced into an oxygen-starved environment, causing explosive ignition of trapped gases. Unlike flashover, a backdraft happens suddenly and without warning.

What are common warning signs of a potential backdraft?

Indicators include yellowish smoke, pulsating windows, and tightly sealed compartments with soot-stained windows.

What strategies can mitigate the risk of flashover and backdraft?

Coordinated ventilation with suppression efforts, maintaining proper timing, and assessing smoke behavior help reduce the risk.

What is a ventilation-controlled fire?

A ventilation-controlled fire occurs when oxygen availability, rather than fuel, determines the fire's intensity and behavior.

Why are ventilation-controlled fires particularly dangerous?

These fires can rapidly intensify when oxygen is introduced, posing a significant risk to firefighters.

What steps should be taken before initiating ventilation during a ventilation-controlled fire?

Attack lines should be established, and water should be applied to the fire's main body before ventilating.

How does wind direction influence ventilation strategies?

Wind can significantly alter smoke movement and fire spread, requiring adjustments to ventilation plans to avoid worsening conditions.

What is the purpose of tactical ventilation in firefighting?

Tactical ventilation aims to improve visibility, reduce heat, and direct smoke away from occupants or escape routes.

How can thermal imaging cameras assist firefighters in ventilation strategies?

Thermal imaging identifies heat sources, fire location, and smoke movement patterns, enhancing decision-making during ventilation efforts.

Why is communication critical during ventilation operations?

Effective communication ensures ventilation teams coordinate with suppression crews, preventing premature or unsafe ventilation actions.

How does building layout impact ventilation effectiveness?

Compartmentalized structures may trap heat and smoke, while open layouts can accelerate fire spread, requiring tailored ventilation approaches.

What are the key factors to consider when determining ventilation timing?

Factors include fire location, smoke movement, readiness of attack lines, and the presence of potential backdraft conditions.

Why is continuous training important for mastering ventilation tactics?

Ongoing training sharpens decision-making skills, improves recognition of fire conditions, and enhances coordination between firefighting teams.

Chapter 7: Flashover and Backdraft

Flashover and backdraft are critical events in fire dynamics that pose significant risks to both firefighters and the structures they aim to protect. Understanding these phenomena is not merely academic but a vital part of ensuring safety and effectiveness in firefighting operations. Both involve rapid fire progression, yet they arise from different conditions and require distinct responses. In every scenario, the ability to recognize the warning signs of flashover and backdraft can mean the difference between life and death. The importance of this knowledge calls for a comprehensive examination of each phenomenon, emphasizing their mechanisms and the observable signs that precede them.

In this chapter, we delve deeper into what causes flashovers and backdrafts, providing insights into how these dangerous scenarios develop. We will explore the particular conditions that contribute to each, such as heat buildup and oxygen deprivation, alongside identifying visual and tactical cues that signal an impending transition. By dissecting these factors, the chapter aims to equip firefighters with the necessary skills to anticipate these events before they fully unfold. Additionally, discussions will cover strategic measures on preventing and mitigating the risks associated with these phenomena through effective ventilation, cooling techniques, and modern instrumentation. These approaches are informed by the latest advancements in fire dynamics research, offering practical guidance to enhance firefighting safety and efficiency.

Understanding Flashover and Backdraft

Flashover and backdraft are two significant phenomena in fire dynamics that every firefighter must understand due to their perilous nature and the unique challenges they present.

Flashover is a rapid and dangerous transition from a developing fire to a fully developed one. It occurs when all combustibles within an enclosure reach ignition temperatures almost simultaneously, resulting in a burst of flames that engulf the entire space. This state marks a pivotal escalation in a fire's lifecycle, where temperature hikes dramatically, often soaring beyond 1,000 degrees Fahrenheit within moments. Such intense heat can have devastating effects, shattering windows and compromising structural integrity.

Several conditions contribute to flashover occurrences. High temperatures, excessive heat buildup, and limited ventilation are primary factors. In an enclosed environment, heat radiates back into the room, rapidly increasing the temperature until the point of ignition for all combustible materials. The feedback loop created by thermal radiation significantly raises the risk of flashover as it continuously adds energy to the contents of a room. Limited ventilation exacerbates this condition by trapping heat and smoke, fostering an environment primed for simultaneous ignition.

Backdraft, on the other hand, arises from a different set of circumstances. It occurs when a fire within an oxygen-deprived setting receives a sudden influx of fresh air, typically through the opening of a door or window. The result is an explosive ignition of accumulated unburnt gases meeting the new oxygen supply. Unlike flashover, which is driven by temperature, backdraft is predominantly an air-driven event. The explosive nature of backdraft makes it particularly hazardous, capable of causing structural damage and posing severe risks to firefighters and occupants alike.

Understanding the specific mechanisms leading to each phenomenon can significantly enhance firefighting strategies. For instance, recognizing the signs of impending flashover—such as visible layers of darkening smoke or intense heat radiating through protective gear—can prompt firefighters to alter their tactics, focusing on ventilation or strategically using water to cool the environment and prevent total ignition. Similarly, awareness of potential backdraft conditions necessitates careful control of ventilation. Recognizing indicators like dense smoke puffing at intervals or glass windows displaying soot patterns can allow responders to take preemptive actions to manage air introduction safely.

The differences between these phenomena underscore the importance of precise identification in emergency scenarios. Misinterpreting flashover signs as backdraft warnings—or vice versa—could lead to inappropriate or hazardous firefighting techniques. Thus, rigorous training and experience are crucial in equipping firefighters with the skills needed to detect early indicators and apply suitable strategies effectively.

Given the dangers associated with both flashover and backdraft, continuous education and practice remain essential. Firefighters must be well-versed in modern firefighting approaches that incorporate insights into these complex fire behaviors. By understanding the science behind flashover and backdraft, firefighting teams can better protect themselves and the communities they serve, ensuring that response efforts minimize risks while maximizing efficiency and safety.

Comprehensive knowledge about flashover and backdraft, supported by advancements in fire dynamics research, has revolutionized firefighting practices. Agencies now employ sophisticated tools like thermal imaging cameras to detect high-risk conditions without directly exposing personnel to potential hazards. Moreover, integration of real-time data analysis allows for dynamic decision-making on the ground, improving the overall safety of firefighting operations.

Differentiating Between Flashover and Backdraft

In the world of firefighting, understanding the nuanced differences between flashover and backdraft is crucial for safety and effective fire management. These two phenomena, though both dangerous and often conflated, are distinct in their mechanisms and consequences. A keen comprehension of these differences can drastically improve a firefighter's ability to respond appropriately and mitigate risks efficiently.

Flashover and backdraft differ primarily in their triggering mechanisms. Flashover occurs when all combustibles within a given space reach their ignition temperature almost simultaneously, resulting in a rapid transition from localized burning to widespread involvement of materials in the room. This phenomenon generally unfolds during the growth phase of a fire, driven by high temperatures and substantial heat buildup. The entire room becomes uniformly hot, with temperatures soaring to levels that allow every flammable item to ignite nearly at once, enveloping the space in flames (Ken, 2024).

Contrastingly, a backdraft involves an explosive event caused by the sudden introduction of oxygen into an environment that was previously starved of it. In a backdraft scenario, a fire has reached an oxygen-deprived state where unburned fuel gases accumulate. The abrupt reintroduction of air, typically due to opening a door or breaking a window, can create a volatile mixture that ignites violently. This explosion is both powerful and destructive, posing immediate danger not only to firefighters but also to the structural integrity of buildings (Tsai & Chiu, 2013).

The outcomes of these phenomena are as different as their initiators. While flashover leads to the complete involvement of combustibles, creating a fully developed fire, backdraft results in a violent explosion that can cause significant damage and spread fire rapidly through pressure waves. Appreciating this distinction helps firefighters tailor their approach to managing these events effectively.

Recognizing the signs that precede each of these occurrences is paramount. For flashover, indicators might include increasing smoke density, high temperatures noticeable even outside the involved area, and rollover—when flames start to appear in the upper levels of smoke (Ken, 2024). Meanwhile, detecting a potential backdraft requires awareness of conditions like thick yellowish smoke, pulsing smoke movement, windows showing dark soot patterns, and an apparent lack of visible flaming combustion inside the compartment. Recognizing these warning signs can help prevent tragic outcomes by allowing for timely interventions.

Given the perilous nature of these events, guidelines on identifying warning signs and adopting safe approaches are vital. Firefighters must develop skills to discern smoke colors and movements, assess building ventilation states, and measure heat levels accurately. For example, understanding that a shift from lighter to darker smoke could signify deteriorating conditions is essential for making informed decisions on advancing or withdrawing safely (Ken, 2024).

Mitigating the risk of both flashover and backdraft during operations involves strategic practices. Ensuring proper ventilation at the right moment can be pivotal in preventing backdrafts, while techniques such as staying low in a potential flashover zone can reduce exposure to extreme temperatures. Using thermal imaging tools helps in identifying heat buildups and gas concentrations, providing a real-time assessment that aids firefighters in adapting their tactics accordingly.

Training plays a critical role in equipping firefighters to handle flashovers and backdrafts. Regular drills focusing on recognizing and responding to these phenomena can significantly enhance situational awareness and decision-making. Moreover, modern technology such as advanced breathing apparatus and protective gear offers additional layers of safety, helping firefighters withstand the harsh conditions imposed by both flashovers and backdrafts (Tsai & Chiu, 2013).

Preventive and Mitigation Tactics for Firefighters

Mitigating the risks associated with flashover and backdraft is crucial for firefighter safety and operational success. Flashover, the rapid ignition of all combustible materials in a space, necessitates prompt intervention to prevent devastating outcomes. Firefighters often employ a set of specialized tactics such as rapid cooling, ventilation control, and the use of thermal imaging cameras to manage these risks effectively.

Rapid cooling involves the targeted application of water to reduce temperatures quickly, thereby preventing the buildup of heat that can lead to a flashover. This technique is typically accomplished using short bursts of water aimed at the ceiling or walls to cool them efficiently without disturbing the thermal layers excessively. Ventilation control plays an equally vital role. By managing airflow into a burning structure, firefighters can manipulate conditions to slow fire spread and decrease temperatures. This practice involves strategic opening and closing of doors, windows, or roof vents to direct smoke and hot gases out of the building safely. Often, this requires precise coordination among team members to ensure that fresh oxygen does not inadvertently accelerate fire growth (Staff, 2008).

Thermal imaging cameras are indispensable tools for modern firefighting, providing critical insights in environments where visibility is limited. These devices enable firefighters to detect thermal signatures and identify potential hotspots even through dense smoke, thus allowing for timely interventions before a flashover occurs. The real-time data from thermal imaging supports decision-making by helping crews allocate resources efficiently and prioritize their actions according to immediate risks.

Understanding and recognizing the warning signs of backdraft is another key strategy in risk mitigation. Backdraft occurs when a fire smoldering in an oxygen-deprived environment suddenly receives fresh air, leading to a rapid explosive reaction. Critical warning signs such as pulsing smoke, significant pressure buildup, and window soot patterns provide cues to anticipating backdraft conditions (*How Do You Deal with Backdraft When Fighting a Fire?*, n.d.). Firefighters must be vigilant in identifying these indicators to adapt their approach accordingly.

One effective method for mitigating backdraft risks is managing ventilation in a controlled manner similar to strategies used for flashover. By creating openings carefully, such as cutting a hole in the roof, firefighters allow built-up gases to escape gradually, reducing the likelihood of an explosive event upon re-entry of oxygen. It is vital that no additional openings on lower floors are made until the vertical ventilation is adequately established, as emphasized by experts in firefighting circles (Staff, 2008).

Strategic planning and communication are cornerstone elements in reducing the dangers posed by both flashover and backdraft. Formulating a clear plan that includes pre-designated escape routes ensures that all team members are aware of safe egress points should conditions rapidly deteriorate. Effective communication is equally important, requiring constant updates between teams operating inside and those coordinating external efforts. This flow of information allows teams to adjust tactics dynamically based on changing circumstances, ensuring that all personnel remain informed about evolving risks.

Moreover, training sessions often simulate these complex scenarios to prepare firefighters for real-life events. Hands-on drills help to reinforce teamwork and cultivate intuitive decision-making skills essential for operating under high-stress conditions. By practicing various techniques in controlled environments, firefighters gain confidence in implementing rapid cooling, ventilation management, and backdraft identification protocols in actual emergencies.

Continuous education on fire dynamics and the latest technological advancements further empowers firefighters to combat these phenomena more effectively. Staying updated with research findings and emerging technologies ensures that teams can leverage the best available tools and methods. As the understanding of fire behavior evolves, integrating new knowledge into tactical approaches becomes paramount.

Concluding Thoughts

Understanding the complexities of flashover and backdraft is imperative for any firefighter committed to safety and effective fire management. This chapter has delved into both phenomena's distinct characteristics, emphasizing the triggers and consequences that differ significantly between them. Flashover involves a rapid ignition of all combustibles when temperatures peak within an enclosed space, leading to a fully developed fire scenario. Conversely, backdraft occurs due to a sudden influx of oxygen in a previously starved environment, causing a violent, explosive reaction with devastating potential. By comparing these events side-by-side, we see the necessity of accurately identifying their signs to tailor firefighting strategies effectively.

Recognizing the warning cues associated with flashover and backdraft can dramatically impact decision-making and response tactics. For example, noticing smoke behavior, temperature shifts, and ventilation conditions can guide whether to apply rapid cooling, manage airflow, or execute controlled ventilation. The integration of these insights into daily firefighting practices, complemented by rigorous training and modern technology, enhances preparedness and minimizes risks. Continuous education on these dynamics enables firefighters to adapt swiftly, ensuring safer outcomes for themselves and their communities when confronting flashovers and backdrafts.

Chapter 7 Test Questions and Answers

What is a flashover in firefighting?

A flashover is a rapid transition from a developing fire to a fully developed fire, where all combustibles in an enclosed space ignite simultaneously due to extreme heat.

What is a backdraft in firefighting?

A backdraft occurs when a fire in an oxygen-deprived environment suddenly receives fresh air, causing an explosive ignition of accumulated gases.

Why is understanding flashover and backdraft crucial for firefighters?

Recognizing the signs of these events can mean the difference between life and death, enabling firefighters to take appropriate measures to prevent or mitigate them.

What is the primary factor driving a flashover?

A flashover is driven by extreme heat buildup, which causes all combustible materials in the room to ignite almost simultaneously.

What is the primary factor driving a backdraft?

A backdraft is driven by a sudden influx of oxygen into an oxygen-deprived environment filled with unburned gases.

What environmental conditions contribute to a flashover?

High temperatures, excessive heat buildup, and limited ventilation.

What are the visual warning signs of an impending flashover?

Dense, dark smoke layers, intense heat radiating through protective gear, and rollover (flames appearing in the upper smoke layers).

What environmental conditions contribute to a backdraft?

An oxygen-deprived fire environment with accumulated unburned gases.

What are the visual warning signs of an impending backdraft?

Thick yellowish smoke, pulsing smoke movement, soot-covered windows, and no visible flame inside the compartment.

How can smoke behavior indicate a potential flashover or backdraft?

Dense, dark smoke layers with rollover suggest flashover, while pulsing smoke with soot-stained windows indicates backdraft.

How can firefighters prevent a flashover?

Using rapid cooling techniques by applying short bursts of water to ceilings and walls to reduce heat buildup.

How can firefighters prevent a backdraft?

Managing ventilation by creating controlled openings to allow gases to escape gradually.

Why is ventilation control important in firefighting?

Proper ventilation slows fire spread, reduces heat buildup, and minimizes the risk of backdraft.

What role do thermal imaging cameras play in fire prevention?

They detect heat buildup and potential flashover or backdraft conditions through dense smoke, improving firefighter safety.

Why is coordination crucial when ventilating a fire scene?

Poor coordination may inadvertently introduce oxygen, accelerating fire growth or triggering a backdraft.

What should firefighters do if they detect flashover warning signs?

Apply cooling techniques, improve ventilation, and retreat to safer areas if conditions deteriorate.

What should firefighters do if they detect backdraft warning signs?

Avoid opening doors or windows until controlled ventilation has been established to release trapped gases safely.

Why is staying low in a potential flashover zone recommended?

The coolest air is closer to the floor, reducing exposure to extreme heat.

What safety equipment can enhance firefighter protection during flashover or backdraft conditions?

Thermal imaging cameras, protective gear, and breathing apparatus improve situational awareness and personal safety.

How does continuous training improve firefighter response to flashovers and backdrafts?

Hands-on drills build muscle memory, improve teamwork, and enhance decision-making in high-stress situations.

Chapter 8: Advanced Fire Behavior Concepts

Understanding advanced concepts in fire behavior is essential for any firefighter aiming to excel in their field. The unpredictable nature of fire makes it a formidable adversary, and grasping these complex dynamics can drastically enhance firefighting strategies and outcomes. Modern tools and technologies, alongside foundational knowledge of building design and materials, are pushing the boundaries of what we know about fire behavior. This chapter delves into these sophisticated elements, offering crucial insights into how they collectively impact fire dynamics. By engaging with this material, readers will deepen their understanding of the mechanisms that influence fire growth and spread, preparing them for real-world challenges.

This journey through advanced fire behavior begins with an exploration of cutting-edge modeling and simulation technologies. These tools are transforming our predictive capabilities, providing invaluable forecasts that aid in decision-making during fire incidents. From there, the discussion moves to the critical role of building design and construction in influencing fire propagation. Readers will learn about the implications of modern materials and architectural methods on fire safety, especially as they contrast with traditional techniques. Finally, the chapter highlights emerging technologies that stand to redefine firefighting approaches. Through drones, robotics, and innovative sensing equipment, firefighters now have unprecedented means to combat fires efficiently while enhancing safety protocols. This chapter equips you with a comprehensive view of these advancements, emphasizing their significance in contemporary fire management practices.

Fire Modeling and Simulation

In the field of firefighting, leveraging computational tools for predicting fire growth and spread has become an indispensable strategy in managing the complexities of modern fire incidents. The ability to anticipate how a fire will behave can drastically improve response times and strategies, ultimately safeguarding lives and property. This subpoint dives into the merits and applications of these advanced technologies, detailing their impact on fire dynamics prediction, firefighter training, real-time decision-making, and preparedness enhancement.

One of the primary applications of computational tools is predicting fire dynamics by using sophisticated software to simulate various scenarios. These simulations are crucial in understanding how fires might evolve under different conditions, accounting for variables such as wind speed, humidity, and terrain. Advanced software like FDS (Fire Dynamics Simulator) is at the forefront of this innovation. Developed by the National Institute of Standards and Technology, it applies Computational Fluid Dynamics (CFD) to model the spread of fire accurately. However, a significant limitation of these tools is their demanding computational requirements, often requiring substantial processing power and time. Despite these challenges, the potential for near-real-time predictions offers critical insights that could transform firefighting strategies (*Framework of a Computer Simulation Tool for Real-Time Command and Control Use to More Effectively Combat Wildfires, 01-R6302*, 2024).

Moreover, these computational models are instrumental in training firefighters by creating realistic simulations of fire events. This approach enables training scenarios that replicate the conditions firefighters may face in actual incidents. By immersing trainees in these virtual scenarios, they gain invaluable experience in navigating complex situations without the risk associated with live exercises. By employing software like FLAMMAP, which integrates semi-empirical models developed by the United States Department of Agriculture Forest Service, trainers can simulate various fire behaviors, providing a comprehensive learning platform. Such tools allow trainees to experiment with different tactics, understand the consequences of their decisions, and refine their skills in a controlled environment.

The utility of computational models extends beyond training, playing a critical role in supporting real-time decision-making during active fire incidents. With actionable insights derived from these models, firefighting teams can make informed strategic decisions swiftly. During an incident, models provide data on fire progression, allowing commanding officers to allocate resources effectively, prioritize evacuation routes, and protect key assets. This capability to adapt strategies based on real-time analysis significantly enhances operational effectiveness, enabling a proactive rather than reactive approach to firefighting. Additionally, integrating satellite data, weather updates, and ground observations ensures a dynamic and responsive model that aids in accurate decision-making throughout the incident's duration (*Framework of a Computer Simulation Tool for Real-Time Command and Control Use to More Effectively Combat Wildfires, 01-R6302*, 2024).

Continuous refinement and validation of these models are essential to enhancing preparedness for future incidents. As our understanding of fire behavior evolves and new technologies emerge, these models must be consistently updated to reflect current knowledge and capabilities. This iterative process involves incorporating feedback from recent fire events, analyzing new research findings, and harnessing innovations in machine learning and data analytics. Such advancements present opportunities to develop more refined models capable of predicting intricate fire behaviors with greater accuracy. For instance, deep learning techniques can analyze historical fire data to identify patterns and refine predictive algorithms, offering insights into potential fire growth mechanisms and improving overall reliability (Ghodrat et al., 2022).

Guidelines for using models in training and real-time decision-making emphasize the balance of realistic replication and adaptability. Training programs should continuously integrate feedback and new scenarios to maintain relevance and rigor. In real-time applications, ensuring that decision-making processes are flexible enough to incorporate dynamic data inputs is vital for effective management of fire incidents. By harmonizing these elements, computational tools serve not only as predictive instruments but also as integral components of comprehensive fire management strategies.

Impact of Building Design and Construction

In recent years, modern building practices have significantly influenced fire behavior, necessitating a reevaluation of traditional firefighting techniques. One critical concern is the increased use of synthetic building materials, which can accelerate fire spread considerably compared to more conventional options like wood or stone. Understanding these materials' combustibility is essential for anticipating how quickly a fire might propagate through a structure and devising effective containment strategies.

Synthetic materials, while offering benefits like cost efficiency and design flexibility, often lack the same level of fire resistance as their traditional counterparts. For instance, lightweight cladding used in many high-rise buildings has been linked to several catastrophic fires globally due to its flammability (Thevega et al., 2022). Historical incidents, such as the Grenfell Tower fire, underscore the urgency to understand and mitigate the risks associated with these materials. Firefighters must be aware of the specific challenges posed by synthetics, particularly regarding ignition and rapid flame spread.

Another important element in modern construction impacting fire dynamics is the fire-resistance ratings of materials and structures. These ratings indicate how long a component can withstand exposure to fire before failing structurally. Such data is crucial for firefighters when assessing how much time they have to work within a burning building safely. It also informs building designs that prioritize safety by incorporating materials capable of maintaining integrity under fire conditions. Ensuring that all materials meet stringent fire-resistance criteria during construction is not just a regulatory requirement but a life-saving measure.

Integrating engineering solutions into architecture is another promising approach to reducing fire risk. This can involve designing buildings with inherent fire prevention mechanisms, such as automatic sprinkler systems, smoke alarms, and compartmentalization to prevent fire spread (Meacham, 2022). Architects and engineers now frequently incorporate these solutions into blueprints, resulting in buildings that are better equipped to handle fire emergencies. Moreover, innovative design features like internal and external fire barriers can significantly slow down fire progression, giving occupants more time to evacuate and emergency responders more time to act.

Comprehensive building codes also play a pivotal role in mitigating fire hazards. By enforcing stringent standards on material selection, construction techniques, and fire protection systems, building codes ensure that new constructions are resilient against fire outbreaks. However, the introduction of modern construction methods, such as prefabrication and modular building, sometimes complicates compliance with traditional codes. These methods often feature challenges like void spaces that can facilitate fire and smoke spread if not adequately addressed (Meacham, 2022). Thus, continuous updates and modifications in building regulations are necessary to keep pace with evolving construction technologies.

Fire prevention through building codes and design considerations should not just be guidelines but integral parts of the construction process from conception to completion. Guidelines should stress regular inspections and maintenance of active fire protection systems, ensuring that they remain operational at all times. For existing buildings, retrofitting with modern fire-resistant materials and technologies can enhance safety without necessitating complete structural overhauls.

To truly grasp how modern building practices affect fire behavior, it is imperative to conduct comprehensive assessments throughout the building's lifecycle, from initial design to post-construction evaluation. This requires close collaboration between builders, architects, engineers, and fire safety experts to create environments that inherently reduce fire risk. By integrating advanced modeling techniques and simulations during the design phase, potential vulnerabilities can be identified and rectified before construction begins.

Emerging Technologies in Firefighting

In the evolving landscape of firefighting strategies, the integration of advanced technologies is transforming the way fires are managed and combated. One such breakthrough is the deployment of drones, which have emerged as invaluable tools in providing aerial perspectives and real-time data on active fire zones. As these unmanned aerial vehicles can reach altitudes and areas that are perilous or inaccessible for humans, they deliver critical visuals and information to ground teams. Drones are equipped with high-resolution cameras and sensors, allowing them to survey large expanses and pinpoint critical zones quickly. According to Justin Baxter, a National UAS Operations Specialist with the Forest Service, drones prove particularly advantageous in situations where thick smoke hinders manned aircraft operations, such as nighttime or high-wind conditions (Networks, 2022).

Complementing drones, the use of thermal imaging and infrared technology plays a pivotal role in detecting hidden hotspots within fire-affected regions. These technologies excel at locating heat sources, even when flames are not visible. By integrating thermal cameras with drones, firefighters gain an enhanced capability to monitor areas more effectively. This synergy was notably significant during the monitoring of wildfires in Oregon, where infrared cameras facilitated accurate identification of burning points amidst vast wooded landscapes (Networks, 2022). This ability allows first responders to focus efforts on the most critical areas, prioritizing actions that could mitigate the spread and intensity of fires.

Robotics further enhance the operational capacity in high-risk environments, such as industrial fires or chemical spills. Firefighting robots, like those discussed in FDNY's robotics program, maneuver through hazardous scenarios that are unsafe for human intervention. Equipped with nozzles, blades, and winches, these machines offer a robust response option for combating fires from a strategic distance. While remote manipulation of these robots presents some challenges, technological advancements are making these units increasingly user-friendly and effective (Horn, 2024). The utilization of robotics not only safeguards human life but also enables extended operational reach in disaster response, demonstrating transformative potential in urban settings and beyond.

Beyond the tactical application of these technologies, leveraging them contributes significantly to efficient resource allocation and improved firefighter safety. With real-time data accessible through drone surveillance and sensor networks, command centers can make informed decisions swiftly. Advanced AI-supported sensor networks, such as Dryad's Silvanet, integrate IoT and artificial intelligence to monitor environmental factors like temperature and humidity. This system provides rapid alerts, enabling proactive measures before fires escalate beyond control (Networks, 2022). Consequently, firefighting teams can allocate resources more strategically, directing manpower and equipment precisely where they are most needed.

Moreover, these technologies bolster firefighter safety by reducing direct exposure to dangerous conditions. With drones and robotics handling reconnaissance and initial assessment tasks, human personnel can focus on implementing calculated interventions. During complex emergencies, this division of labor ensures that responders remain out of harm's way until the situation is fully understood and controlled. By relying on technological precision, fire departments minimize risks and enhance their overall efficiency in battling blazes.

As we traverse deeper into an era shaped by both complex fire behavior and innovative solutions, it becomes clear that investing in cutting-edge technologies is indispensable for modern firefighting. From delivering a bird's-eye view over unfolding crises to ensuring swift detection of threats via infrared capabilities, these advancements represent tangible assets in safeguarding communities. The ongoing research and development in this field underscore a commitment to embracing innovation as an ally against one of nature's most formidable forces.

Final Insights

Understanding advanced fire behavior concepts through modeling, building design and construction, and emerging technologies equips firefighters with vital tools for modern-day challenges. This chapter explored how computational models are used to predict fire dynamics, train firefighters, and assist in real-time decision-making. These technologies enhance situational awareness and allow for better preparation and response strategies by simulating various scenarios and integrating feedback from real events. Additionally, the impact of synthetic building materials on fire spread and resistance ratings were discussed, highlighting the need for continuous updates and improvements in building codes and construction practices to ensure safety.

Emerging technologies like drones, thermal imaging, and robotics have revolutionized firefighting tactics, providing real-time data and reducing human exposure to dangerous conditions. The integration of AI-supported sensor networks further enhances decision-making capabilities by monitoring environmental factors and offering rapid alerts. These advancements underscore the importance of leveraging technology to safeguard communities effectively. By understanding these complex elements, firefighters can employ a proactive approach in combating fires, ensuring both efficiency and safety in their operations.

Chapter 8 Test Questions and Answers

What is the primary benefit of using computational tools in firefighting?

Computational tools help predict fire growth and spread, improving response times and strategies to safeguard lives and property.

Which software is commonly used for modeling fire dynamics, and who developed it?

The Fire Dynamics Simulator (FDS) developed by the National Institute of Standards and Technology is widely used.

What is a major limitation of computational fire modeling tools like FDS?

They require significant processing power and time to generate accurate predictions.

How does FLAMMAP contribute to firefighter training?

FLAMMAP simulates various fire behaviors, allowing trainees to experience realistic fire scenarios and test different strategies safely.

Why is real-time decision-making enhanced by fire modeling tools?

These tools provide actionable insights, enabling commanders to allocate resources, prioritize evacuation routes, and protect key assets effectively.

What role does integrating satellite data and weather updates play in fire modeling?

It ensures models are dynamic, adjusting to changing conditions for improved decision-making.

How can machine learning improve fire modeling?

By analyzing historical data, machine learning refines predictive algorithms, improving accuracy in forecasting fire behavior.

What is a key recommendation for improving fire modeling training programs?

Training programs should regularly integrate new scenarios and feedback to maintain relevance.

Why is adaptability important when using fire modeling tools during active incidents?

Real-time models must incorporate dynamic data inputs to respond effectively to changing fire conditions.

How can continuous refinement of computational models enhance preparedness for future fires?

By incorporating lessons from past incidents and advancing algorithms, models become more precise and reliable.

How do synthetic materials impact fire behavior compared to traditional materials?

Synthetic materials can accelerate fire spread more quickly than conventional options like wood or stone.

What is the significance of fire-resistance ratings in construction materials?

These ratings indicate how long a material can withstand fire exposure before structural failure.

Why is lightweight cladding a fire concern in modern high-rise buildings?

Lightweight cladding is highly flammable and has been linked to catastrophic fires like the Grenfell Tower incident.

How can compartmentalization in building design improve fire safety?

By dividing a structure into fire-resistant sections, compartmentalization slows fire spread and provides safer evacuation routes.

What construction challenge arises from prefabricated and modular building methods?

These methods can create void spaces that facilitate the spread of fire and smoke if not properly managed.

What role do building codes play in improving fire safety?

Building codes enforce material standards, construction techniques, and fire protection systems to enhance fire resilience.

How can retrofitting existing buildings improve fire safety?

Adding modern fire-resistant materials and updated fire protection systems can enhance safety without extensive structural changes.

Why should fire assessments be conducted throughout a building's lifecycle?

Regular assessments identify vulnerabilities from design to post-construction, ensuring continued fire resilience.

How do drones improve firefighting strategies?

Drones provide aerial perspectives and real-time data, enhancing situational awareness and guiding resource allocation.

What advantage does thermal imaging provide in firefighting?

Thermal imaging detects hidden hotspots, helping firefighters target critical areas even in low-visibility conditions.

Chapter 9: Post-Incident Analysis and Learning

Post-incident analysis and learning are essential for enhancing firefighting strategies. Understanding how incidents unfold allows firefighters to develop effective tactics that address specific challenges posed by different fire scenarios. This chapter dives into the intricacies of analyzing events after they occur, emphasizing the vital role such evaluations play in crafting not only responsive but also proactive firefighting strategies. The process is aimed at capturing first-hand experiences and translating them into robust lessons that can be shared across teams, promoting continuous improvement and adaptation within the field. By systematically reviewing past incidents, firefighters can recognize patterns and make informed predictions about future occurrences, leading to more efficient and safer operations.

In this chapter, readers will explore a comprehensive approach to scrutinizing and learning from firefighting incidents. It begins with a focus on debriefing sessions, which facilitate open dialogue among team members regarding their experiences and insights. Recognizing both successes and areas needing refinement is crucial, as it challenges individuals to view each incident as an opportunity for growth. A significant portion of the discussion also revolves around leveraging collected data to inform training programs. These programs are crafted to incorporate real-world examples, ensuring that firefighters are equipped with practical knowledge and skills necessary for tackling complex fire dynamics. Additionally, the chapter highlights the importance of creating feedback loops to ensure new learnings continuously enrich operational strategies. With advances in technology, tools like simulation frameworks offer enhanced insights, enabling departments to model potential outcomes and refine approaches accordingly. Through these collective efforts, the chapter underscores a culture of collaboration and relentless pursuit of excellence in firefighting.

Debriefing and Lessons Learned

Analyzing fire behavior is crucial for improving firefighting tactics, and it begins by systematically reviewing specific incidents to identify patterns. This approach requires a detailed examination of past fires to uncover recurring behaviors that can guide future tactical decisions. When firefighters understand how certain types of fires behave under specific conditions, they can anticipate and counteract potential threats more effectively.

A systematic review process involves collecting detailed data on various aspects of each incident. Key elements include the fire's origin, the materials involved, weather conditions, and the time of day. By comparing these variables across different incidents, firefighters can begin to discern patterns and trends. These insights are invaluable for developing more refined strategies tailored to diverse fire scenarios. The goal is to equip firefighters with the knowledge needed to make informed decisions quickly and confidently during emergencies.

To facilitate this learning, debriefing sessions play an essential role. After-action reviews provide a structured environment where team members can share their experiences and observations. Debriefings aren't merely about recounting actions taken but delving into what worked, what didn't, and why. They create an opportunity to gather firsthand accounts from those directly involved, offering a wealth of practical insights and firsthand experiences. These sessions should emphasize areas needing improvement while also recognizing innovations that have proven effective.

Debriefings allow leaders to collect diverse perspectives, leading to a holistic understanding of each incident. Firefighters often encounter unique challenges in the field; thus, sharing these experiences helps the entire team learn from one another. Furthermore, encouraging open and honest communication during debriefings fosters a culture of continuous learning and adaptation. It's vital for teams to feel safe discussing mistakes or uncertainties without fear of judgment, as this openness leads to genuine growth and progress.

However, gathering information is only the first step. The real challenge lies in transforming these insights into actionable training programs. Developing a feedback loop is crucial for ensuring that lessons learned from past incidents inform and enhance future responses. This feedback loop integrates new knowledge into existing training curricula, thereby fostering ongoing tactical advancement.

Training programs should be dynamic, reflecting the latest findings from incident analyses. Incorporating real-world examples and case studies into training sessions can significantly enhance their relevance and effectiveness. By simulating situations based on actual events, firefighters can better prepare for similar occurrences, honing their skills in a controlled environment. Additionally, incorporating scenario-based training exercises allows team members to experiment with different strategies and techniques, evaluating their efficacy before deploying them in real-life situations.

The feedback loop not only focuses on technical skills but also addresses leadership and decision-making capabilities. Understanding fire behavior patterns is vital, but equally important is knowing how to respond decisively under pressure. Training programs should incorporate elements that test and develop critical thinking, problem-solving, and communication skills. By doing so, firefighters can cultivate a well-rounded skill set that prepares them to tackle the multifaceted challenges posed by modern fire incidents.

As part of this continuous learning cycle, it's important to adapt and update training materials regularly. New technologies, tools, and methods are constantly evolving in the firefighting industry. Ensuring that training programs reflect these advancements keeps firefighters at the forefront of innovation. Additionally, soliciting feedback from participants after training sessions helps identify areas for further improvement, making subsequent iterations even more effective.

Sharing Knowledge and Best Practices

In the world of firefighting, one critical element for success lies in enhancing departmental performance through effective knowledge sharing. The very nature of firefighting demands a constant evolution of strategies and tactics, as each incident presents unique challenges. Hence, sharing experiences, successes, and lessons learned across the department can significantly improve overall efficiency and safety.

Establishing an open platform within the department where all members can contribute their experiences and insights is a vital step towards this goal. Such a platform fosters an environment where team members feel valued and motivated to share their firsthand experiences. This collaborative approach not only helps in capturing tacit knowledge—those unwritten skills and insights that experienced firefighters have—but also inspires innovative ideas that may lead to improved tactics and decision-making processes. By having a structured environment for sharing, departments can better preserve valuable knowledge and avoid the risk of it being lost when team members retire or move on. This is particularly beneficial for capturing insights on rare but critical incidents that new recruits might not encounter frequently.

Mentorship structures play an equally important role in facilitating the transfer of knowledge from seasoned veterans to newer recruits. Firefighting is steeped in tradition, with much of its knowledge passed down orally from generation to generation. Formalizing this process through mentorship programs ensures this rich heritage is preserved while bringing fresh perspectives into the mix. Experienced firefighters can offer practical advice, historical context, and nuanced understanding of fire dynamics that cannot be gleaned from textbooks alone. On the other hand, newer recruits often bring new energy and modern techniques that can rejuvenate traditional practices. This symbiotic relationship promotes a culture of continuous learning and adaptation, key in maintaining high-performance levels within the department. As Source 1 states, mentoring can be significantly more cost-effective than formal training sessions (Winstanely, 2021).

The documentation and distribution of effective strategies and successes in a centralized database accessible to all department members complete the loop of knowledge sharing. This repository acts as a living source of information, continually updated with the latest learnings from various emergencies. It ensures that everyone from veteran firefighters to administrative staff can access and benefit from compiled expertise, thus creating a communal knowledge base. This database can include detailed case studies of significant incidents, summaries of post-incident debriefings, and even multimedia resources such as training videos or simulations.

Furthermore, a central database allows for a review of past challenges and how they were overcome, turning them into teaching moments for future scenarios. Organizing these experiences into actionable data makes it easier for departments to identify patterns and potential areas for improvement. For example, if certain strategies consistently yield positive outcomes during specific firefighting scenarios, they can be formally integrated into the department's standard operating procedures.

For the database to be effective, consistent updating and management are necessary. This responsibility can be distributed among members, encouraging a sense of ownership and active participation in knowledge retention efforts. Additionally, this approach minimizes silos within the department by promoting cross-functional collaborations, fostering transparency, and building trust—key elements in any successful firefighting operation.

After-Action Reports

In firefighting, the importance of analyzing past incidents cannot be overstated. Evaluating these incidents provides critical insights that can lead to enhanced safety and more effective future operations. One of the primary ways to do this is through the detailed documentation of fire behavior observations. This practice allows firefighters and their agencies to understand precisely how fires act under different conditions. Comprehensive recordings can serve as valuable references for training and operational planning.

Documentation of fire behavior should include variables like weather conditions, building materials involved, and the spread pattern of the fire. These records help create a repository of knowledge that informs current and future tactical decisions. By understanding trends from past fires, firefighters can predict how new fires might behave, allowing them to prepare appropriately and react promptly, thereby improving outcomes. As noted by Carr (2024), handling the unexpected becomes more manageable when there is a framework of prior knowledge to rely upon.

A parallel focus is necessary on analyzing firefighter actions during incidents. Understanding decision-making processes and outcomes helps in evaluating what works and what doesn't in live situations. This requires a culture of openness where mistakes are seen as learning opportunities rather than failures. When firefighters closely analyze their responses, they can identify strengths and weaknesses in their approach. For example, decision-making models that stress quick assessments and immediate action may need refinement if data indicates a pattern of poor outcomes or inefficiencies. As suggested by Cardil et al. (2021), sharpening situational awareness involves integrating real-time data with lessons learned from prior incidents, leading to improved decision-making during emergencies.

Moreover, identifying success stories and challenges faced during firefighting operations aids in refining and bolstering future strategies.

Successful case studies serve as motivational tools and provide concrete examples of effective tactics. On the other hand, acknowledging challenges encourages an environment of continuous improvement. This dual approach ensures that strategies evolve based on real-world experiences, leading to more robust operational protocols.

It is also beneficial to incorporate technological advancements into post-incident evaluations. Tools such as fire simulation frameworks allow for modeling potential outcomes based on historical data, offering predictive insights that can be invaluable in strategizing resource allocation and tactical positioning (Cardil et al., 2021). These simulations offer a risk-free environment to test new theories and refine existing methods, thereby enhancing preparedness and response effectiveness.

To fully leverage the potential of incident analysis, it's essential to foster a supportive and collaborative departmental culture. Encouraging open dialogue among team members about past incidents can uncover hidden insights and promote shared learning. Teams should routinely debrief after incidents, discussing both successes and areas for improvement. This practice encourages transparency and collective growth, which benefits everyone involved.

Further, capturing these discussions in a formalized way ensures that the knowledge is not lost over time. Creating an accessible database of past incident analyses allows all department members to draw from a rich pool of wisdom accumulated through various experiences. This centralized knowledge base can inform everything from daily drills to large-scale strategic planning.

In summary, evaluating firefighting incidents thoughtfully and systematically opens up avenues for significant improvements in strategies and safety protocols. By documenting fire behavior meticulously, analyzing firefighter actions critically, and identifying patterns of success and challenge, fire departments can enhance their operations continuously. The integration of technology further amplifies these efforts, offering new dimensions to traditional analysis methods.

Lessons Learned

As we draw conclusions from this chapter, the importance of enhancing firefighting strategies through comprehensive analysis and shared learning emerges as a pivotal theme. By systematically examining past incidents, firefighters can identify patterns in fire behavior that inform tactical decisions. This meticulous review process, complemented by detailed debriefing sessions, equips teams with valuable insights into both successful strategies and areas needing improvement. Sharing these lessons within departments fosters a culture of openness and continuous adaptation, where honest communication allows for genuine growth. It's evident that learning from experience is not only foundational but also transformative in refining firefighting tactics to address diverse challenges effectively.

Moreover, creating dynamic training programs rooted in real-world examples and integrating them with feedback loops reinforces ongoing tactical advancement. These programs should embrace new technologies and scenario-based exercises that reflect the latest findings, thereby preparing firefighters for future incidents. The cultivation of leadership and decision-making skills remains crucial, ensuring firefighters are well-rounded in their approach to modern fire incidents. Central to this mission is an environment that prioritizes knowledge sharing and mentorship, bridging the gap between seasoned veterans and newer recruits. As departments continuously update training materials, they remain at the forefront of innovation, fostering a more effective response to emergencies.

Chapter 10: Effective Firefighting Strategies

Effective firefighting strategies are fundamental to safeguarding lives and property during fire emergencies. At their core, these strategies encompass a comprehensive understanding of fire behavior, continuous and rigorous training, and fostering a culture centered around safety. By mastering these components, firefighters enhance their ability to respond swiftly and decisively in the face of unpredictable and dangerous fires. The complexities of firefighting demand an approach that integrates knowledge, skill, and vigilance, adapting to evolving scenarios with informed precision. This chapter delves into the critical elements that form the backbone of successful firefighting operations, underscoring the significance of being well-prepared and adaptable in high-stakes situations.

In this chapter, we explore the multifaceted nature of effective firefighting strategies, beginning with a thorough examination of fire behavior. Understanding how fires grow, spread, and interact with different environmental conditions is crucial for making strategic decisions during incidents. We will delve into the various stages of fire development, highlighting how each phase presents unique challenges and opportunities for intervention. Additionally, the chapter will discuss the vital role of regular training and preparedness exercises, which equip firefighters with the skills and confidence needed to perform under pressure. Furthermore, the importance of fostering a robust safety culture within fire departments will be addressed, emphasizing the need for teamwork, clear communication, and continuous learning. Through this exploration, readers will gain insight into the essential practices that empower firefighters to protect communities effectively.

The Importance of Understanding Fire Behavior

Understanding fire behavior is crucial for effective firefighting, offering the foundation upon which strategic decisions are made during a fire incident. At its core, fire behavior examines how fires grow, propagate, and are impacted by environmental conditions, and it's this study that equips firefighters with the knowledge needed to respond quickly and effectively.

Fire development is a vital concept within fire behavior. It involves understanding the stages a fire undergoes as it grows. Each stage of fire development presents distinct characteristics and challenges, thus recognizing these stages aids firefighters significantly. For instance, the incipient stage features a fire just beginning to ignite, often manageable if caught early. As the fire progresses to the growth stage, it becomes more intense, requiring swift action to prevent further spread. Understanding when a fire enters its peak intensity at the fully developed stage can dictate rigorous suppression actions. Finally, the decay stage indicates a reduction in available fuel, yet hazards such as re-ignition due to remaining embers remain present. Knowing these transitions helps firefighters choose appropriate suppression techniques, whether that means using water to cool down surfaces or implementing ventilation strategies to reduce smoke build-up. This awareness enables them to tackle fire scenarios with precision and efficiency.

In addition to developmental stages, numerous factors influence how a fire behaves, each necessitating consideration during firefighting operations. Fuel type stands as one of the primary variables affecting fire behavior. Materials such as wood, synthetic fibers, and metals burn differently, influencing the intensity and speed of a fire's spread. For example, synthetic materials common in modern buildings may release energy at a higher rate, complicating firefighting efforts with faster-spreading and hotter fires. Recognizing the type of fuel involved allows for tailored approaches, such as determining the necessity for specific extinguishing agents or tactical ventilation.

Topography plays another significant role in fire behavior, shaping fire paths and velocities. Fires tend to move uphill faster, driven by preheated air and flames rising along slopes. This kind of movement can dictate the deployment of resources and personnel to areas most likely affected by advancing flames. Acknowledging these geographical influences ensures firefighters anticipate potential fire paths, positioning themselves strategically to maximize their effectiveness.

Weather conditions intimately affect fire behavior, altering its dynamics significantly. Wind acts as both an amplifier and guide, fostering rapid directional shifts and intensification. High winds can transform small fires into uncontrollable blazes with overwhelming speed, demanding immediate adaptations in firefighting tactics. Furthermore, temperature and humidity levels also impact the ease of ignition and subsequent fire spread, with drier conditions heightening flammability. Firefighters must continually assess weather forecasts and on-the-ground changes to inform their decisions, seeking windows of opportunity to safely approach and suppress the blaze.

Moreover, assessing potential hazards before and during fire incidents is essential for optimal resource allocation and decision-making. Hazards such as proximity to explosive materials or the presence of toxic substances require specialized handling and protective measures. Identifying such risks early allows responders to coordinate with hazardous materials teams and employ specialized equipment, minimizing health risks and maximizing safety. By assigning resources accordingly, firefighters ensure effective containment and mitigation, while safeguarding both themselves and the public.

Resource allocation based on hazard assessment is critical during active fire incidents. When confronting large-scale fire situations, decisions must be made swiftly regarding where to direct manpower and tools. For instance, protecting human life and critical infrastructure often takes precedence, directing emergency response toward residential areas or industrial plants. Strategic deployment ensures that available resources produce the greatest impact, maintaining control over rapidly evolving situations.

Constant assessment and adaptation form the backbone of successful firefighting operations. Given the dynamic nature of fires, static strategies seldom suffice. Instead, continuous evaluation of fire conditions and behaviors enables firefighters to adapt their methods efficiently. In practice, this means observing changes in flame length, smoke density, or heat output to infer shifts in fire stages or behavior. Using such real-time observations, incident commanders can modify tactics, adjusting things like hose streams or ventilation points to better align with current conditions.

Firefighters must approach every scene with a mindset of adaptability, prepared to pivot their strategies as required. Engaging in frequent post-incident analyses fosters learning from past experiences, enhancing readiness for future emergencies. These reviews offer insights into effective practices and highlight areas for improvement, contributing to the ongoing refinement of firefighting strategies.

Ultimately, comprehending fire behavior goes beyond theory, manifesting in practical applications that enhance firefighting efficacy. It underscores the importance of preparedness, training, and research within the field, all aimed at refining our understanding and response capabilities. By embracing this knowledge, firefighters position themselves as informed, proactive protectors against one of nature's most formidable forces. Continual education and collaboration with researchers contribute to the evolution of firefighting tactics, ensuring we keep pace with changing fire dynamics and environmental contexts.

Preparedness and Training for Firefighter Safety

In the face of unpredictable and dangerous fires, preparedness and training form the backbone of firefighter safety. Regular drills play a crucial role in simulating real-life scenarios that firefighters may encounter in dynamic and high-risk situations. These drills are designed to mirror the chaotic nature of actual fire incidents, allowing firefighters to practice their skills and refine their responses in a controlled environment. The simulated conditions help them become adept at making quick decisions under pressure, a skill vital for maintaining composure and effectiveness during actual emergencies.

Training also includes comprehensive instruction on the use of personal protective equipment (PPE), which is essential for safeguarding firefighters from various hazards. PPE serves as the first line of defense against chemical, thermal, and physical dangers inherent in firefighting. By mastering the correct use and maintenance of gear such as helmets, gloves, and turnout suits, firefighters can significantly reduce their risk of injury. This aspect of training not only emphasizes the importance of protection but also instills confidence in firefighters, knowing they are well-equipped to handle the hazardous environments they face.

Another critical component of effective firefighting is developing teamwork and communication skills. High-pressure environments require seamless coordination among team members to ensure successful operations. Firefighting is inherently a collaborative effort, where each member's role is interdependent on others. Teamwork training focuses on enhancing communication protocols, such as using radios and other devices for clear instructions and feedback. It also entails understanding and executing the incident command system, which standardizes roles and responsibilities during emergencies. Through these practices, firefighters learn to trust and rely on one another, fostering an atmosphere of mutual support and efficiency.

Continuous evaluation of training programs is equally vital. By regularly assessing the effectiveness of current training methods, fire departments can identify areas that need improvement or updating. Evaluations often incorporate performance assessments, peer feedback, and self-reflections to gain insights into both individual and team capabilities. These evaluations act as a foundation for refining existing protocols and introducing innovative safety procedures, ensuring firefighters remain up-to-date with best practices and emerging challenges.

The integration of realistic simulations, thorough PPE training, strong teamwork, and ongoing program evaluations do more than prepare firefighters for emergencies; they cultivate a culture of safety and learning within the fire service. Staying updated with the latest fire behavior research is critical, as it provides a scientific basis for improving tactics and strategies. Similarly, engaging in regular drills helps refresh and test the knowledge gained, cementing skills and increasing readiness.

Fostering a culture of safety goes beyond training; it involves creating an environment where continuous learning is encouraged and prioritized. Firefighters are often faced with new and evolving threats, necessitating an adaptable mindset and a commitment to lifelong education. Encouraging participation in specialized workshops and courses allows firefighters to explore advanced techniques and innovative approaches, promoting skill enhancement and professional growth.

Real case studies and experiences shared by seasoned firefighters add a valuable dimension to training sessions, providing firsthand insights into the complexities of firefighting. Learning from past incidents helps in understanding the nuances of fire dynamics and enhances problem-solving abilities. Moreover, it reinforces the impact of efficient preparation on mission success and personal safety.

Fire services should also establish partnerships with research institutions and emergency management organizations. These collaborations can lead to evidence-based policy development, ensuring that the strategies employed are informed by the latest findings and technologies. Partnerships encourage a constant exchange of knowledge and resources, ultimately supporting the goal of improved firefighter safety and efficiency.

Ongoing Education and Research

In the ever-evolving landscape of firefighting, continuous education and research stand as crucial pillars for advancing strategies and enhancing safety. As fire dynamics continue to change with environmental and technological advancements, staying updated with the latest studies offers firefighters cutting-edge tools to tackle new challenges effectively. The integration of contemporary scientific insights into fire behavior equips personnel with a deeper understanding, thus enabling more informed decision-making on the field.

Firefighters must regularly engage with new developments in their field to maintain an edge over unpredictable fire behavior. They can achieve this by consistently participating in specialized workshops and courses that are designed to foster skill enhancement and innovation. Such educational forums provide an avenue to explore novel techniques and methods which can be immediately applied to practical situations. These programs not only refresh existing knowledge but also introduce innovative approaches that enhance tactical decisions and operational efficiency. Through structured learning opportunities, firefighters gain exposure to the latest tools and methodologies, ensuring they remain at the forefront of firefighting excellence.

Moreover, establishing partnerships with research institutions forms the backbone of evidence-based policy development within the firefighting community. Collaborations with academic researchers open avenues for applying scientific rigor to real-world problems, leading to more effective and safer firefighting techniques. By leveraging the expertise of research bodies, fire departments can incorporate empirical findings into training programs and operational protocols, significantly reducing risks associated with fire-related incidents. This synergy between field operations and academic research ensures a constant flow of up-to-date knowledge, fostering a proactive approach towards emerging fire hazards.

The importance of cultivating a learning-oriented culture within fire services cannot be overstated. Such a culture promotes resilience and adaptability, essential qualities in high-stakes environments. Encouraging continuous learning and professional development instills confidence among firefighters to embrace new technologies and methodologies. Departments that prioritize education and training create an atmosphere where personnel are motivated to seek out knowledge actively, contributing to a more dynamic and responsive firefighting force.

To further advance firefighting strategies and safety, integrating modern technology into regular training is fundamental. Digital platforms like the Fire Safety Academy provide invaluable resources for translating complex fire science into actionable strategies (*Fire Safety Academy | the Fire Safety Research Institute (FSRI), Part of UL Research Institutes*, 2024). These platforms offer firefighters access to tailored courses that accommodate individual learning styles and schedules, facilitating ongoing education without disrupting daily responsibilities.

Additionally, collaborations in technology and product development play a pivotal role in improving firefighter safety. By working with tech developers and researchers, fire departments can assess the practicality and effectiveness of new safety equipment and technologies. This collaboration ensures that innovations are not only theoretically sound but also practically viable, enhancing situational awareness and reducing response times during emergencies (<i>Fire Prevention & Safety Grants - Research & Development | FEMA.gov</i>, n.d.).

Furthermore, the creation and implementation of database systems contribute significantly to identifying trends and predictors related to firefighter injuries. Systematic data collection allows for a comprehensive analysis of various factors influencing safety outcomes, from demographic aspects to health metrics. Access to such information enables departments to tailor training and safety measures according to specific needs, ultimately diminishing injury rates and promoting well-being among firefighters (<i>Fire Prevention & Safety Grants - Research & Development | FEMA.gov</i>, n.d.).

Ultimately, advocating for continued education and research in firefighting does more than just update knowledge; it transforms the entire approach to managing fires. By embracing a culture of learning and integrating scientific advancements into everyday practices, firefighters not only enhance their skills but also contribute to crafting a safer work environment. Future strategies will heavily rely on the ability to adapt to new information and incorporate findings from diverse fields, fundamentally shifting the paradigm of traditional fire service operations.

Final Thoughts

Understanding fire behavior, continuous training, and fostering a culture of safety are indispensable pillars of successful firefighting. By grasping how fires develop and behave, firefighters gain crucial insights that guide their actions in real time, allowing for precise and effective decision-making. This understanding is further strengthened through simulation and hands-on training, where firefighters hone their skills and learn to navigate the unpredictable nature of fires with agility and confidence. Personal protective equipment training and teamwork exercises affirm this preparedness, ensuring each firefighter is not only well-equipped but also capable of functioning seamlessly within a coordinated team. These elements collectively form the foundation upon which safer and more efficient firefighting operations are built.

The ongoing commitment to education and research amplifies these efforts, empowering firefighters to adapt swiftly to evolving challenges. Staying informed about new fire dynamics and technologies equips them with innovative strategies that enhance both individual and team responses to emergencies. By fostering collaboration with research institutions and engaging continuously in professional development, fire departments maintain a proactive stance against emerging hazards. This dedication to lifelong learning ensures that every member is prepared, adaptable, and ready to protect communities effectively. Embracing these comprehensive practices, firefighters are better positioned to confront the formidable force of fire, safeguarding lives and properties while upholding a steadfast commitment to safety and excellence.

References List

Fire Safety In High-Risk Settings | American Trade Mark Co. (2024). American Trade Mark Co. https://www.firecommand.org/fire-safety-in-high-risk-settings/?srsltid=AfmBOooW2jMl81p26-bFRs4QIY1b1OhqFVuTaP9Zi2fmuefvBOtyMKLS

Liu, Z., Liu, H., Azmi, N. F., & Farid Wajdi Akashah. (2024, October 1). *A dynamic risk assessment model for evacuation in healthcare facilities during fire scenarios.* Journal of Building Engineering; Elsevier BV. https://doi.org/10.1016/j.jobe.2024.111129

Thompson, K. D. (2010, November 17). *Fire Dynamics.* NIST. https://www.nist.gov/el/fire-research-division-73300/firegov-fire-service/fire-dynamics

Unlocking the Secrets of Fire Behavior: A Vital Evolution in Firefighting Tactics. (2024, January 23). https://www.fireengineering.com/firefighting/unlocking-the-secrets-of-fire-behavior-a-vital-evolution-in-firefighting-tactics/

20North. (2024, April 9). *What is a Fire Tetrahedron? | 4 Components of Fire.* Hazard Control Technologies. https://hct-world.com/what-is-a-fire-tetrahedron/

Blazequel. (2024, February 21). *The fire triangle: Understanding the three components of fire.* Blazequel.com. https://blazequel.com/blog/the-fire-triangle-understanding-the-three-components-of-fire/

University of South Carolina. (2019). *The Fire Triangle.* Sc.edu. https://www.sc.edu/ehs/training/Fire/01_triangle.htm

wfca_teila. (2023, September 19). *Carbon Emissions from Wildfires: What You Need to Know | WFCA.* WFCA. https://doi.org/10948433649/85HzCOzp7OIDEPGtz-Qo

Chaudhry, A. (2024, April 10). *The Four Stages Of Fire And When To Call For Help.* Element Fire Extinguishers. https://elementfire.com/blogs/articles/the-four-stages-of-fire-and-when-to-call-for-help?srsltid=AfmBOorfcvhry1X0lL3PexPvGKwyg_K4o34eckSt9msG_8kQ5

Rielage, R. (2024, October 16). *4 steps of sound fireground decision-making.* FireRescue1. https://www.firerescue1.com/leadership/4-steps-of-sound-fireground-decision-making

Scheviak, T. (2021, January 6). *What are the Different Stages of a Fire?* Www.firetrace.com. https://www.firetrace.com/fire-protection-blog/different-stages-of-a-fire

Science Learning Hub. (2009, November 19). *Fire behaviour.* Science Learning Hub; Science Learning Hub. https://www.sciencelearn.org.nz/resources/763-fire-behaviour

UCAR/COMET. (2024). *MetEd» Sign In.* Ucar.edu. https://www.meted.ucar.edu/fire/s290/unit1/print.php

wfca_teila. (2024, May 7). *Fire Incident Command System: Your Ultimate Guide.* WFCA. https://wfca.com/preplan-articles/incident-command-system/

Extreme Fire Behavior: Understanding the Hazard. (2018, April 8). Extreme Fire Behavior: Understanding the Hazard | CTIF - International Association of Fire Services for Safer Citizens through Skilled Firefighters. https://www.ctif.org/news/extreme-fire-behavior-understanding-hazard

Ken. (2024, November 10). *The Critical Difference Between Flashover and Backdraft.* Firerescue.com.au; Fire Rescue Classifieds. https://www.firerescue.com.au/the-critical-difference-between-flashover-and-backdraft

Understanding Heat Transfer: A Guide for Fire Investigators | Warren Forensics. (n.d.). Www.warrenforensics.com. https://www.warrenforensics.com/2024/02/21/understanding-heat-transfer-a-guide-for-fire-investigators/

Unlocking the Secrets of Fire Behavior: A Vital Evolution in Firefighting Tactics. (2024, January 23). https://www.fireengineering.com/firefighting/unlocking-the-secrets-of-fire-behavior-a-vital-evolution-in-firefighting-tactics/

Ashenhurst, S. (2018, May 31). *The Leap-frog Effect: Protecting tall buildings from exterior fire spread.* Construction Specifier. https://www.constructionspecifier.com/the-leap-frog-effect/

Courses | National Advanced Fire & Resource Institute. (2024). Nafri.gov. http://www.nafri.gov/courses

Fire Safety Training: A Comprehensive Guide. (n.d.). SafetyCulture. https://safetyculture.com/topics/fire-safety/fire-safety-training/

Loudermilk, E. L., O'Brien, J. J., Goodrick, S. L., Linn, R. R., Skowronski, N. S., & Hiers, J. K. (2022, June 10). *Vegetation's influence on fire behavior goes beyond just being fuel.* Fire Ecology. https://doi.org/10.1186/s42408-022-00132-9

Williams, F. A. (1977, January 1). *Mechanisms of fire spread.* Symposium (International) on Combustion. https://doi.org/10.1016/S0082-0784(77)80415-3

admin. (2024, April 10). *Fire Behaviour Prediction Under Specific Conditions & Factors.* Ken Institute. https://keneducation.in/fire-behaviour-prediction-under-specific-conditions-factors/

| *Compartment Fire Behavior.* (n.d.). https://cfbt-us.com/wordpress/

Navarro, K. (2020, December). *Working in Smoke:* Clinics in Chest Medicine. https://doi.org/10.1016/j.ccm.2020.08.017

Staff, F. (2008, September 30). *The Impact of Negative Pressure.* FirefighterNation: Fire Rescue - Firefighting News and Community. https://www.firefighternation.com/firefighting/the-impact-of-negative-pressure/

Staff, F. E. (2021, January 3). *Ventilation-Limited Fire: Keeping it Rich and Other Tactics Based Off Science.* Fire Engineering. https://www.fireengineering.com/firefighting/ventilation-limited-fire-keeping-it-rich-and-other-tactics-based-off-science/

» *Tactical Ventilation | Compartment Fire Behavior*. (2014). Cfbt-Us.com. https://cfbt-us.com/wordpress/?tag=tactical-ventilation&paged=3

Ventilation-Limited Fires and the Influence of Oxygen - Fire Engineering: Firefighter Training and Fire Service News, Rescue. (2017, June 22). https://www.fireengineering.com/firefighting/ian-bolton-ventilation-limited-fires-and-the-influence-of-oxygen/

FLASHOVER AND BACKDRAFT: A Primer. (2005, March 1). Fire Engineering. https://www.fireengineering.com/firefighting/flashover-and-backdraft-a-primer/

How do you deal with backdraft when fighting a fire? (n.d.). FireRescue1. https://www.firerescue1.com/backdraft/articles/how-do-you-deal-with-backdraft-when-fighting-a-fire-CAVezT4ixOUMHyxR/

Ken. (2024). *The critical difference between flashover and backdraft. Fire Rescue Classifieds*. Retrieved from https://www.firerescue.com.au/the-critical-difference-between-flashover-and-backdraft/amp/

Ken. (2024, November 10). *The Critical Difference Between Flashover and Backdraft*. Firerescue.com.au; Fire Rescue Classifieds. https://www.firerescue.com.au/the-critical-difference-between-flashover-and-backdraft

Staff, F. (2008, August). *Understanding, Anticipating & Avoiding Flashover*. FirefighterNation: Fire Rescue - Firefighting News and Community. https://www.firefighternation.com/training/understanding-anticipating-avoiding-flashover/

Tsai, L. C., & Chiu, C. W. (2013, May). *Full-scale experimental studies for backdraft using solid materials*. Process Safety and Environmental Protection. https://doi.org/10.1016/j.psep.2012.05.007

Framework of a Computer Simulation Tool for Real-Time Command and Control Use to More Effectively Combat Wildfires, 01-R6302.

(2024, March). Southwest Research Institute. https://www.swri.org/work-us/internal-rd/2023/chemistry-materials/01-r6302

Ghodrat, M., Shakeriaski, F., Fanaee, S. A., & Simeoni, A. (2022, December 31). *Software-Based Simulations of Wildfire Spread and Wind-Fire Interaction*. Fire. https://doi.org/10.3390/fire6010012

Horn, M. (2024, October 14). *InnovateEnergy*. InnovateEnergy. https://innovateenergynow.com/resources/fdnys-robotics-program-enhancing-fire-safety-through-innovation

Meacham, B. J. (2022). *Fire performance and regulatory considerations with modern methods of construction*. Buildings and Cities. https://doi.org/10.5334/bc.201

Networks, D. (2022, December 16). *Climate change technologies to tackle wildfires*. Dryad. https://www.dryad.net/post/climate-change-technologies-to-help-tackle-wildfires

Thevega, T., Jayasinghe, J. A. S. C., Robert, D., Bandara, C. S., Kandare, E., & Setunge, S. (2022, December). *Fire compliance of construction materials for building claddings: A critical review*. Construction and Building Materials. https://doi.org/10.1016/j.conbuildmat.2022.129582

Cardil, A., Monedero, S., Schag, G., de-Miguel, S., Tapia, M., Stoof, C. R., Silva, C. A., Mohan, M., Cardil, A., & Ramirez, J. (2021, October 1). *Fire behavior modeling for operational decision-making*. Current Opinion in Environmental Science & Health. https://doi.org/10.1016/j.coesh.2021.100291

Carr, B. (2024, November 15). *Thinking Firefighters: The Theory Behind the Action - Fire Engineering*. Fire Engineering: Firefighter Training and Fire Service News, Rescue. https://www.fireengineering.com/firefighting/structural-firefighting/thinking-firefighters-the-theory-behind-the-action/

Tolg, B., & Lorenz, J. (2020, October 9). *An analysis of movement patterns in mass casualty incident simulations*. Advances in Simulation. https://doi.org/10.1186/s41077-020-00147-9

Winstanely, G. (2021, October 28). *Using Mentoring for Knowledge Transfer & Sharing - Mentorloop.* Mentorloop Mentoring Software. https://mentorloop.com/blog/mentoring-knowledge-transfer-sharing/

Wildland Fire Leadership Levels, Leadership Committee | NWCG. (2024, November 12). NWCG. http://www.nwcg.gov/committee/leadership-committee/leadership-levels

eLearning Company Blog. (2024, July 29). *Improving Performance through Knowledge Management and...* The ELearning Blog; eLearning Company, Inc. https://elearning.company/blog/improving-performance-through-knowledge-management-and-sharing/

Fire Safety Academy | The Fire Safety Research Institute (FSRI), part of UL Research Institutes. (2024). Fsri.org. https://fsri.org/programs/fire-safety-academy

Fingal, J. (2022, January 18). *Fire Behavior.* Extension Communications. https://extension.oregonstate.edu/catalog/pub/em-9341-fire-behavior

Fire Prevention & Safety Grants - Research & Development | FEMA.gov. (n.d.). Www.fema.gov. https://www.fema.gov/grants/preparedness/firefighters/safety-awards/research-development

Holm, C. (2023, November 20). *Behind the Scenes: A Day in the Life of a Firefighter.* Fire Force. https://www.fforce.com/blogs/articles/behind-the-scenes-a-day-in-the-life-of-a-firefighter?srsltid=AfmBOorBDnx0gl3aYNGfhfGI3katKPP_vbt0i1RId3

Staff, F. E. (2023, November 8). *All In: Maximizing Team Strengths for Better Fire Department Performance.* Fire Engineering: Firefighter Training and Fire Service News, Rescue. https://www.fireengineering.com/firefighting/all-in-maximizing-team-strengths-for-better-fire-department-performance/

Unlocking the Secrets of Fire Behavior: A Vital Evolution in Firefighting Tactics. (2024, January 23).

https://www.fireengineering.com/firefighting/unlocking-the-secrets-of-fire-behavior-a-vital-evolution-in-firefighting-tactics/

About the Author

Eric J. Neal is a Fire Chief and Emergency Management Director with a Master's in Public Administration and a Bachelor's in Emergency Management. He has served in departments across Texas and Tennessee, sharing his expertise through mentorship and education. His first year as Fire Chief inspired this book, offering lessons for leaders in fire service.

www.ingramcontent.com/pod-product-compliance
Lightning Source LLC
Chambersburg PA
CBHW071204130726
47998CB00002B/608